10 QUICK QUESTIONS A DAY

THIS BOOK BELONGS TO

_____

Year 4 | Term 1

Acknowledgements and Copyright Laws

Lizard Learning Pty Ltd
GPO Box 1941, Brisbane, Queensland, 4001
ABN: 13 158 235 333
www.lizardlearning.com

Copyright © Lizard Learning
Reprinted 2023
Reprinted 2017
First published and printed 2015

Publisher: Lizard Learning Pty Ltd
Content Writers: Cindy Holmberg-Smith, Carmen Kliendienst, Barbara Stewart, Cassandra Potts, Elizabeth Beames
Content Editors: Cindy Holmberg-Smith, Carmen Kliendienst, Barbara Stewart, Steven Fay
Digital Formatter: New Wave Design, Natalie Pugsley
Cover Design: Book Cover Cafe, New Wave Design
Illustrators: Trevor Salter, Book Cover Cafe, Aleisha Coffey, New Wave Design
Project Managers: Cindy Holmberg-Smith, Anthony Puttee
Administration Officers / Desktop Operators: Natalie Pugsley, Dylan Holmberg

Reproduction and communication for educational purposes
The Australian Copyright Act 1968 (the Act) allows for maximum of one chapter or 10% of the pages of work, whichever is the greater, to be reproduced and/or communicated by any educational institution for its educational purposes provided that the educational institution (or the body that administers it) has given remuneration notice to Copyright Agency Limited (CAL) under the Act. For details of the CAL licence for educational institutions contact Copyright Agency Limited (www.copyright.com.au).

Reproduction and communication for other purposes
Except as permitted under the Act (for example a fair dealing for the purposes of study, research, criticism, or review), no part of this book may be reproduced, stored in a retrieval system, communicated or transmitted in any form or by any means without prior written permission. All enquiries should be made to the publisher at the address above.

Classroom Use
This book is an INDIVIDUAL STUDENT WORKBOOK. For teachers to use this workbook in the classroom, please contact sales@lizardlearning.com for a reduced whole class or whole school licence (digital or hard copy). Alternatively, contact your local bookstore to purchase.

This book is not to be treated as a blackline master.

All rights reserved.

ISBN: 978-1-925509-48-9

Year 4

Name: _____

Term 1 - Week 1 - Day 1

1. Rewrite the sentence/s with the correct **punctuation** and **spelling**.
   what would you like for diner tonite mum asked the famly
   _____

2. **A noun is the name of people, places, animals or things.**
   Write the **nouns** in this sentence: The treasure was buried in a chest at the bottom of the deep blue sea. _____

3. **A prefix is a letter or group of letters placed before or in front of a word to change its meaning (e.g. un, re, mis).** Which word has the **prefix** that matches the meaning?
   To not like something.   unlike / dislike / likable _____

4. **Homophones are two or more words that sound the same but have different meanings or spellings (e.g. right / write).** Write a matching **homophone** for **Chile**. _____

5. Write the words you find in this word worm. _____
   _____
   _____
   _____

6. What time does the teacher's clock show right now? _____
   What will be the time **15 minutes** from now? _____
   6 months + 5 months = _____   How many **days** in a **fortnight**? _____

7. How **much** money is shown? 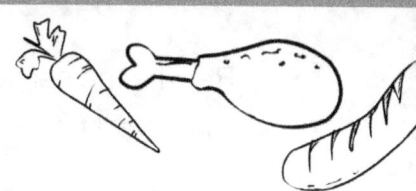 _____
   Spell your answer. _____

8. Complete this **picture pattern**:
   △ ☆ ◯ ____ ____ ◯ ____ ____ ◯ △

9. Using 1 litre, 250 millilitres, 2 litres or 5 litres match the correct **measurement** to each picture:

   ____ L   ____ L   ____ L   ____ mL

10. 80 mountaineers were hiking. They had to walk the difficult trail in groups of ten.
    How many in each group? _____   How many groups? _____

Year 4

Name: _____

Term 1 - Week 1 - Day 2

1. Rewrite the sentence/s with the correct **punctuation** and **spelling**.
   sam luved to do all sorts of execise such as runing jumping and even skiping
   _____
   _____

2. ***Verbs are doing / action words.*** Write the **verb** in this sentence:
   I was pushing my little sister on her favourite yellow swing. _____

3. ***A suffix is a letter or group of letters placed after or at the end of a word to change its meaning.*** Add the correct **suffix** (**-ly, -ion** or **-ed**) to these words.
   believe _____   correct _____
   slow _____   fresh _____

4. ***A homograph is a word that has the same spelling but a different meaning (e.g. fine/fine) and sometimes a different sound (e.g. tear/tear).***
   Which word/s are **homographs?** cheek / block / joyful / change _____

5. Write the **odd** word out: above   below   sideways   fruit   _____

6. What time does the teacher's clock show right now? _____
   What will be the time **10 minutes** from now? _____
   14 months - 12 months = _____ What **day** comes before **Friday**? _____

7. **Draw** 2 shapes to show the **fraction** $\frac{1}{2}$.

8. Who travelled by bus the **most**? _____
   Who **didn't** catch a bus at all? _____

   Number of Days Travelled by Bus in a Fortnight
   (bar graph showing: Amber, Eunice, Rema, Harrison, Chloe, Chelsea, Dyson, Floyd)

9. ***Volume is length x width x height. V = L x W x H. The symbol for cubic centimetres is abbreviated as cm^3*** (e.g. 3cm x 2cm x 7cm = $42cm^3$).
   How many **cubic centimetres** are in this diagram? _____ cm^3

10. The oyster farmer had 609m of oysters growing on 1 plot and 310m on another plot. How many metres of oysters did he have to harvest? _____

Year 4

Name:

Term 1 - Week 1 - Day 3

1. Rewrite the sentence/s with the correct **punctuation** and **spelling**.
   on the holidays josie visited slippery dip aquatic senter fiften times
   _____
   _____

2. **Adjectives are describing words.** Write the **adjectives** in this sentence:
   My brother plays with his blue football every weekend. _____

3. **Plurals are words that mean more than one.**
   Write two **plurals** you would find in a **playground**. _____

4. **Antonyms are words that are opposites.** Write an **antonym** for these words.
   dirty _____   over _____   anyone _____
   rich _____   cloudy _____ please _____

5. Write the **vowels** in the following words:
   b ___ ___ c h   r ___ m ___ m b ___ r ___ d   b ___ f ___ r ___
   b ___ ___ g h t   c ___ m p ___ t ___   b l ___ ___ d

6. What time does the teacher's clock show right now? _____
   What will be the time **20 minutes** from now? _____
   What is the missing **12 hour** time?   3:50   3:55   _____   4:05   4:10
   How many **days** in the **month** of your birthday? _____

7. My answer is 24. I have doubled the first number. What number did I start with?
   Show your work. _____

8. **< means less than   > means greater than**
   2 more than 7 020 is [ ]   2 more than 3 000 + 7 001

9. How many **faces**? _____
   How many **corners**? _____

10. The chicken farmer's shed was 1010 metres long. He sold half of his chickens so he only needed half of the space. How much unused space did he have left?
    _____

Year 4

Name: _____

Term 1 - Week 1 - Day 4

1. Rewrite the sentence/s with the correct **punctuation** and **spelling**.
   the two boys jakets were exactly the same
   _____
   _____

2. ***An adverb is a word which modifies or adds meaning to a verb, adjective, or adverb by telling how, when, why or where a thing is done.*** Find the **adverbs** in this sentence:
   The boy was happily jogging along on the exercise path. _____

3. ***Compound words are two or more words joined together to form a new word (e.g. seashell).*** Write a **compound word** you would find **at the beach**. _____

4. ***Synonyms are words that have similar meanings.*** Write a **synonym** for these words.
   closed _____ seat _____ near _____
   laugh _____ small _____ jet _____

5. Write if these sentences are **past**, **present** or **future tense**.
   I am running home from school today. _____
   I am going to run home from school tomorrow. _____
   I ran home from school yesterday. _____

6. What time does the teacher's clock show right now? _____
   What was the time **20 minutes** ago? _____
   10 months + 12 months = _____
   Before midday or **after** midday? 10:00am _____ 4:10pm _____

7. Write **9263** in words. _____
   _____

8. *Challenge!* Write as a **fraction** the **chance** of the spinner landing on blue.
   _____

9. **Converting metres (m) to centimetres (cm) x 100.**
   Converting centimetres (cm) to metres (m) ÷ 100.
   Convert to **centimetres**:
   2.13m = _____ cm   4.34m = _____ cm

10. In the barn there were 6 chickens. Each chicken had laid 3 eggs, how many eggs were there altogether? _____
    Spell your answer. _____

10 Quick Questions a Day | www.lizardlearning.com

Name: _____

Term 1 - Week 1 - Day 5

1. Rewrite the sentence/s with the correct **punctuation** and **spelling**.
   our footy teem one in the finals between the blewbirds and the rugrats
   _____

2. *A pronoun is a word that takes the place of a noun (e.g. her, him, it, themselves).*
   Write the correct **pronoun** into this sentence:
   I like it when _____ (**them** / **he** / **herself**) tells funny jokes.

3. **Contractions are shortened forms of two words.**
   He's is the **contraction** for the words: _____

4. **There are three articles: the, a and an. The, is a definite article (e.g. give me the cup). A, is an indefinite article (e.g. give me a cup. This would be any cup). An, is the article to use before a vowel (e.g. an umbrella).** List the **article/s** in this sentence:
   A shirt was washed and ironed by the laundry. _____

5. **Rearrange** these words to make a proper sentence: at the pony school when riding We one our were horses frightened. became of _____
   _____

6. What time does the teacher's clock show right now?_____
   What was the time **25 minutes** ago?_____
   11 months - **2 months** = _____   **1 century** = _____ years
   Write the **months** of Summer._____

7. Write the number the **abacus** shows. _____
   Write the number in words. _____
   _____

8. Write the coordinates for the **hexagon**. _____
   Which **shape** is at 4,D? _____

9. Write the **short way**:
   50 grams _____ ,   116 grams _____ .

10. Write an addition number story for the numbers 462 and 214.
    _____
    _____
    _____

10 Quick Questions a Day | www.lizardlearning.com

Year 4

Name:

Term 1 – Week 2 – Day 1

1. Rewrite the sentence/s with the correct **punctuation** and **spelling**.
   that dres is now harf price so i mite by it said renee to melissa
   _____

2. *A phrase is a group of words without a verb. Many phrases start with a preposition.*
   Write the **phrases** in this sentence: The cream was on both layers of the cake.
   _____

3. Correctly rewrite the misspelled words in this sentence:
   It was a suny day so the washing dryd very quikly. _____

4. Write the **nearest meaning** to **broom**. _____
       a) to sip quickly   **b)** to sweep the floor with

5. *Writing Time!* Finish this sentence: The screen door was open, and I was shocked to...
   _____
   _____.

6. What time does the teacher's clock show right now? _____
   What was the time **25 minutes** ago? _____
   Write in the missing **12 hour** times.   5:55   6:55   7:55   _____ _____ _____
   What **angle** does **3pm** show on the clock face? _____

7. Write as **numerals**: five thousand three hundred and four: _____
   six thousand nine hundred and one and two tenths: _____

8. On the compass write **N**, **S**, **E** and **W** in their correct positions.

9. *An acute angle is less than 90 degrees. A right angle is 90 degrees. An obtuse angle is greater than 90 degrees but less than 180 degrees. A straight angle is 180 degrees exactly (a line). A reflex angle is greater than 180 degrees.*
   Which **angle** is the **obtuse** angle? _____ Which are the **acute**? _____
   What **type** of angle is C? _____

     A   B   C   D

10. There were 27 screws and 3 cars needed them for their windshield wipers.
    How many screws were needed for each car? _____

Name: _____

Term 1 – Week 2 – Day 2

1. Rewrite the sentence/s with the correct **punctuation** and **spelling**.
   at swiming lessens we are lerning backstrok frestile butterfli and breststrok
   _____
   _____

2. *A sentence or a clause, is a group of related words containing a subject and a verb.*
   Rearrange these words to make a **clause**: were The playing pool. by children the
   _____

3. **Unjumble** these words. The words in the box are spelled correctly to help you.
   eelebiv _____   ktabse _____
   rsidsate _____   utmnrgae _____

   | believe | disaster |
   | basket | argument |

4. *Homophones are two or more words that sound the same but have different meanings or spellings (e.g. right / write).* Write which of these words are **homophones** and write their partner. witch / past / children _____

5. **Rearrange** these words in **alphabetical** order. _____
   _____

   paw   quite   aboard   medium

6. What time does the teacher's clock show right now? _____
   What will the time be in **30 minutes** from now? _____
   35 months + 3 months = _____ = _____ years _____ months
   What kind of **angle** shows **3:25pm** on a clock face? _____

7. If you had $14.00, would you be able to **buy** the soccer ball? _____
   If not, how **much more** money would you need? _____

8. Complete the **fraction pattern**.
   $\dfrac{35}{100}$ $\dfrac{40}{100}$ $\dfrac{45}{100}$ _____   _____   _____   _____

9. What **day** does the **2nd April** fall on? _____

10. 141 flowers were growing in the front garden and 141 flowers were growing in the back garden. How many flowers did the gardener have to care for? _____

Year 4

Name:

Term 1 - Week 2 - Day 3

1. Rewrite the sentence/s with the correct **punctuation** and **spelling**.
   jacks shirt was staned when he spilt his grap jouce on himselff
   _____
   _____

2. *A preposition is a word used before a noun or a pronoun to show its relationship to some other word in the sentence; it is used to make a phrase (e.g. under the box, in the box, on the box, by, up, down, near, through, over, at).*
   Write the **prepositions** you find in these phrases.
   under the fence _____ in the playground _____

3. *Apostrophe of ownership: for singular words to show possession of one owner, add an apostrophe then the letter s to the owner (e.g. dolphin's tail, Ollie's toothbrush). For plural words, that end in s, to show ownership, add an apostrophe after the s (e.g. teachers' staffroom).* Write the **apostrophe of ownership** in the sentence:
   The girls shoes were new, so one of their toes had a blister. _____

4. *Can you remember the meaning of homographs and homophones to complete this question?* Is **bed** in this sentence a **homograph** or **homophone**?
   Be careful not to run through the flower bed. _____

5. Write the words you find in this word worm. _____
   _____
   _____

6. What time does the teacher's clock show right now? _____
   What was the time **30 minutes** ago? _____
   Before midday or **after** midday?
   10:06am _____   8:05pm _____
   3:19pm _____

Year 4

Term 1 – Week 2 – Day 3

7. This recipe makes 32 muesli bar pieces. Change the recipe to make 16 muesli bar pieces.

2 cups desiccated coconut	_____ desiccated coconut
2 cups unsalted peanuts	_____ unsalted peanuts
2 cups sunflower seeds	_____ sunflower seeds
2 cups sesame seeds	_____ sesame seeds
$1\frac{1}{2}$ cups rolled oats	_____ rolled oats
$\frac{1}{2}$ cup butter	_____ butter
1 cup brown sugar	_____ brown sugar
$\frac{1}{2}$ cup honey	_____ honey

8. Who watched the **most** television?
   _____

   Who watched the **least** television?
   _____

Hours of TV watched in a week by 4C	
Jane	𝍷𝍷𝍷𝍷𝍷 |||
Ali	||
Ronan	𝍷𝍷𝍷𝍷𝍷 𝍷𝍷𝍷𝍷𝍷 ||
Heather	𝍷𝍷𝍷𝍷𝍷
Tanisha	𝍷𝍷𝍷𝍷𝍷	

9. What **time** does group Saturn start drawing? _____

5M's Art Group Timetable for Term One				
Activity	1.00pm	1.30pm	2.00pm	2.30pm
Face Painting - *Mr Beard*	Saturn	Mars	Earth	Neptune
Pottery - *Miss Potter*	Mars	Earth	Neptune	Saturn
Craft - *Mrs Simms*	Earth	Neptune	Saturn	Mars
Drawing - *Ms Curves*	Neptune	Saturn	Mars	Earth

10. Complete this magic square so each row, column and diagonal adds to **69**.

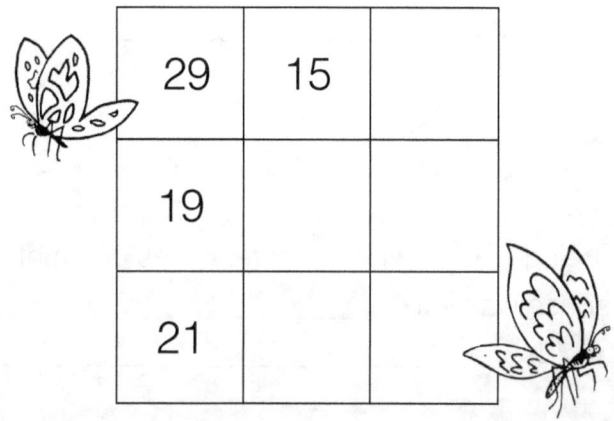

Year 4

Name: _____

Term 1 - Week 2 - Day 4

1. Rewrite the sentence/s with the correct **punctuation** and **spelling**.
   why did the teacher alwayz look at her for the answer wandered christie
   _____
   _____

2. Write the **dictionary** meaning for **cruel**. _____
   _____

3. **A prefix is a letter or group of letters placed before or in front of a word to change its meaning (e.g. un, re, mis).**
   Correctly add a **prefix** to this word (**dis** / **un** / **pre**): _____ agree

4. **Antonyms are words that are opposites.** Think of an **antonym**. Write a sentence with its opposite. Underline the **antonym** used. _____
   _____

5. Write four words. Make one the **odd one** out. *Test someone near you.*
   _____   _____   _____   _____

6. What time does the teacher's clock show right now? _____
   What will be the time **40 minutes** from now? _____
   What are the missing **12 hour** times?   _____   4:30   4:45   5:00   5:15   _____
   How many **months** in **Winter**? _____

7. Find **ten** first then add the other numbers.
   1 emu egg, 2 chicken eggs, 9 duck eggs.
   How many altogether? _____

8. **= equal to   or   ≠ not equal to**
   32 + 29 [ ]   sixty - two   147 [ ]   100 + 47   28 + 12 [ ]   12 + twenty

9. Which lines are **parallel lines**? _____

   A   B   C   D

10. The semitrailer was being loaded with furniture. It was 890 metres long and was half loaded, how much space was left? _____
    Write the answer in words. _____

Year 4 — Term 1 – Week 2 – Day 5

Name: _____

1. Rewrite the sentence/s with the correct **punctuation** and **spelling**.
   that wedding dress was so bewtifool i wood lik the saym won when i get maried
   _____
   _____

2. *A noun is the name of people, places, animals or things.*
   Name four **nouns** you would find **on your street**.
   _____   _____   _____   _____

3. *A suffix is a letter or group of letters placed after or at the end of a word to change its meaning.* Add the **suffix -est** to the best word that makes sense.
   happy _____   table _____   beautiful _____
   Write this new word in a sentence. _____
   _____

4. *Synonyms are words that have similar meanings.*
   Think of four **synonyms**. *Test someone on their knowledge of synonyms that would match!*
   _____ _____   _____ _____
   _____ _____   _____ _____

5. Write the five **vowels**. _____
   Write the **consonants** in **alphabetical** order. _____
   _____

6. What time does the teacher's clock show right now? _____
   What was the time **15 minutes** ago? _____
   26 months + 5 months = _____ = _____ years _____ months
   How many **days** in a **fortnight**? _____ days

7. Write the **numeral** for **three thousand**. _____

8. What is the **chance** your teacher will wear a dress tomorrow?
   impossible, likely, possible or **certain**: _____

9. *Challenge!* Using 1 litre, 50 millilitres, 375 millilitres or 500 millilitres match the correct **measurement** to each picture:

   ____ mL   ____ mL   ____ mL   ____ L

10. The baker had baked 9 meat pies on 7 trays, how many pies had he baked for that day?
    _____ . Write your answer in words. _____

Name:

Year 4   Term 1 – Week 3 – Day 1

1. Rewrite the sentence/s with the correct **punctuation** and **spelling**.
   Ipads come in lots of colurs such as red blak white and yellow but i prefer pink
   _____
   _____

2. **Verbs are doing / action words.** Name four **verbs** you would find **in the library**.
   _____ _____ _____ _____

3. **Plurals are words that mean more than one.**
   Circle the correct **plural** form of **beach**:   beachiss / beaches

4. **There are three articles: the, a and an. The, is a definite article (e.g. give me the cup). A, is an indefinite article (e.g. give me a cup. This would be any cup). An, is the article to use before a vowel (e.g. an umbrella).** Write a sentence that includes one **article**.
   _____

5. Write the **past, present, future tense** of these words.

	Past	Present	Future
teach			
close			
film			
chase			

6. What time does the teacher's clock show right now? _____
   What will be the time **40 minutes** from now? _____
   17 months + 11 months = _____ How many **months** in **2 years**? _____

7. What number are the **MAB blocks** showing? _____

8. Which **shape** is shown at 4,A? _____
   Is the **shape** at 4,B, a 2D or 3D shape? _____

9. **Volume is length x width x height. V = L x W x H.**
   The symbol for cubic centimetres is abbreviated as cm³
   (e.g. 3cm x 2cm x 7cm = 42cm³). Challenge! How many **cubic centimetres** are in this diagram? _____ cm³

10. Write a subtraction number story for the numbers 238 and 327. _____
    _____

Year 4

Name: _____

Term 1 – Week 3 – Day 2

1. Rewrite the sentence/s with the correct **punctuation** and **spelling**.
   the cakes icing was choccolate flavoured so i eight it furst
   _____

2. **Adjectives are describing words.** Write four **adjectives** to describe a **monster truck**.
   _____ _____ _____ _____

3. **Compound words are two or more words joined together to form a new word (e.g. seashell).** Complete these **compound words**.
   cook _____ child _____ gate _____

4. Write the **nearest meaning** to **proud**. _____
           a) to stand tall, a feeling   **b)** to start something new

5. **Rearrange** these words to make a proper sentence: TV were walked through when lizard the open in We a door. watching _____
   _____

6. What time does the teacher's clock show right now? _____
   What will be the time **15 minutes** from now? _____
   What are the missing **12 hour** times? 4:10 4:12 _____ 4:16 4:18 _____
   How many **months** in each **season**? _____

7. Sum of 8 and 9: _____ Product of 2 and 2: _____ One dozen plus six: _____

8. What is the **northern** most city? _____
   What states are **west** of Queensland? _____

9. Which shape is a **triangular based pyramid**?
   _____

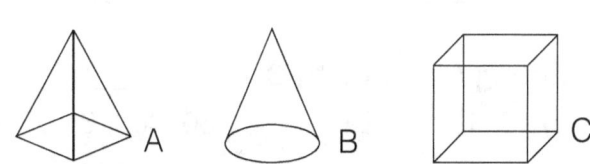

10. Complete this magic square so each row, column and diagonal adds to **111**.

Year 4 — Term 1 – Week 3 – Day 3

Name: _____

1. Rewrite this sentence with the correct **punctuation** and **spelling**.
   allan didnt understand why his dad said he shouldnt walk around the backyard with out shoes untill the day he stood on a prickel _____
   _____

2. *An adverb is a word which modifies or adds meaning to a verb, adjective, or adverb by telling how, when, why or where a thing is done.* Write four **adverbs**.
   _____ _____ _____ _____

3. *Contractions are shortened forms of two words.* Write the **contractions** for:
   we are _____,   they are _____,   we will _____ .

4. *Homophones are two or more words that sound the same but have different meanings or spellings (e.g. right / write).* Write matching **homophones** for these words.
   reign _____ scene _____
   right _____ sleigh _____

5. *Writing Time!* Finish this sentence: My dog had a bone in his mouth and to my surprise he...
   _____
   _____ .

6. What time does the teacher's clock show right now? _____
   What will be the time **50 minutes** from now? _____
   93 months + 2 months = _____   How many? _____ years _____ months

7. Using both numbers and words, write the 2 **fractions** you see below the diagrams.
   _____   _____
   Which **fraction** is bigger? _____

8. Write the group of numbers that shows **counting forwards** by 3's. _____
   a) 68, 70, 72, 74   b) 33, 43, 53, 63   c) 13, 16, 19, 22   d) 3, 30, 300, 3 000 30 000

9. ▬▬▬ Approximate to the nearest **cm** the **length** of this line. _____

10. 84 plums were in a bowl. Throughout the day, 7 people in the office ate the same number each from the bowl. At the end of the day there were none left. How many plums did they eat each? _____

Year 4

Name:

Term 1 - Week 3 - Day 4

1. Rewrite this sentence with the correct **punctuation** and **spelling**.
   michelle was in trouble because her bike tire was flat. she was very far from home and also from school were she was heded _____
   _____
   _____

2. *A pronoun is a word that takes the place of a noun (e.g. her, him, it, themselves).*
   Write the **pronoun/s** you find in this sentence: You and I can either have fish and chips for dinner or eat a salad roll. _____

3. Correctly rewrite the misspelled words. sqare / towards / sandwhich / themselfs
   _____

4. *A homograph is a word that has the same spelling but a different meaning (e.g. fine/fine) and sometimes a different sound (e.g. tear/tear).*
   Provide one example of a **homograph** on **the weekend**: _____

5. Write these words in **alphabetical** order. _____
   _____

   invite   however   stung   pirate

6. What time does the teacher's clock show right now? _____
   What will be the time **55 minutes** from now? _____
   What **angle** does **1:20** show on a clock face? _____

7. *Challenge!* If you bought the shoes and the shirt, how **much** would it cost? _____

   shoes $39.90   dress $78.30   belt $19.95   shirt $60.50

8. Write the **number** for the tally marks shown in this table:

Hours of TV watched in a week by 4C	
Jane	𝍬 IIII
Ali	II
Ronan	𝍬 𝍬 II
Heather	IIII
Tanisha	𝍬 I

9. **Converting kilograms (kg) to grams (g) x 1000.**
   Converting grams (g) to kilograms (kg) ÷ 1000.
   Convert **2 kilograms** to **grams**. _____

10. At the Athletics Carnival there were 316 Year 3 children running in the cross country and 231 Year 4 children. How many children are there running altogether? _____
    Write the answer in words. _____

10 Quick Questions a Day | www.lizardlearning.com

Year 4

Name:

Term 1 - Week 3 - Day 5

1. Rewrite the sentence/s with the correct **punctuation** and **spelling**.
   all the students report cards were handed out on the last da of term_____
   _____

2. **A preposition is a word used before a noun or a pronoun to show its relationship to some other word in the sentence; it is used to make a phrase (e.g. under the box, in the box, on the box, by, up, down, near, through, over, at).** Write four other **prepositions**.
   _____ _____ _____ _____

3. **Unjumble** four spelling words from your weekly class list.
   Test someone to see if they can work out your challenge!
   _____ _____ _____ _____
   _____ _____ _____ _____

4. **Can you remember the meaning of antonyms to complete this question?**
   Write the definition for **antonyms**. _____
   _____

5. Write the words you find in this word worm. _____
   _____

   (word worm containing letters: akdtoward, between, outside, nshare, extelevisiona)

6. What time does the teacher's clock show right now?_____
   What was the time **55 minutes** ago? _____
   What are the missing **12 hour** times?   4:00   5:00   6:00   _____ _____

7. Write out the 2 x tables. Write the **turnaround** beside. Here is an example to start you off.
   First way: *The turnaround way:*
       2 x 0 = 0   _____   0 x 2 = 0   _____
       2 x 1 = 2   _____   1 x 2 = 2   _____

Year 4

Term 1 - Week 3 - Day 5

8. Using the **coordinates N, S, E, W**, fill in the blank:
   New South Wales is _____ of Queensland.

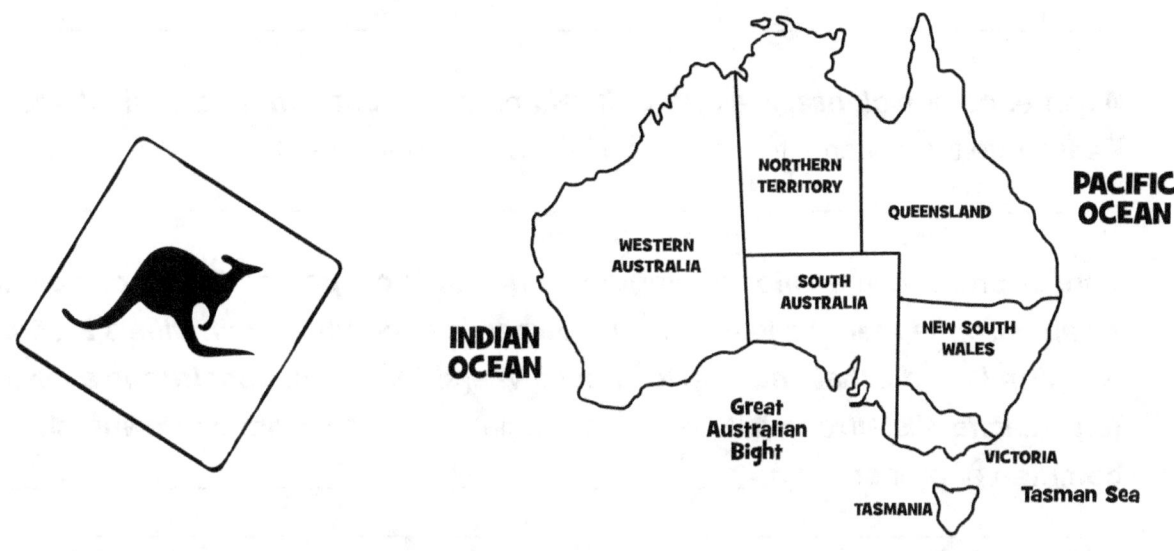

9. *An acute angle is less than 90 degrees. A right angle is 90 degrees. An obtuse angle is greater than 90 degrees but less than 180 degrees. A straight angle is 180 degrees exactly (a line). A reflex angle is greater than 180 degrees.*
   Which **angle** is a **right** angle? _____

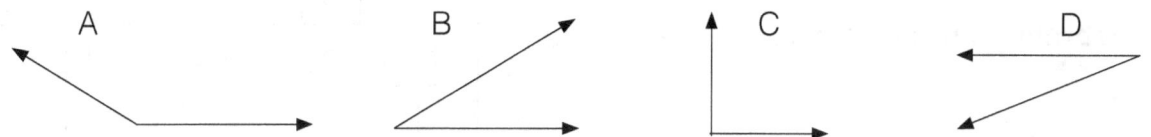

10. Complete this magic square so each row, column and diagonal adds to **186**.

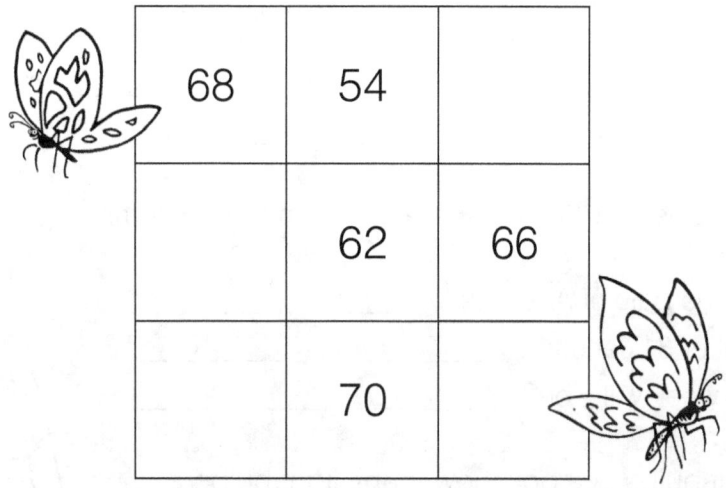

Year 4

Name: _____

Term 1 - Week 4 - Day 1

1. Rewrite the sentence/s with the correct **punctuation** and **spelling**.
   can you think of a froot begining with K askd the teecher
   _____

2. *A sentence or a clause, is a group of related words containing a subject and a verb.*
   Rearrange these words to make a **clause**: Queen sitting her throne. The was on
   _____

3. *Apostrophe of ownership: for singular words to show possession of one owner, add an apostrophe then the letter s to the owner (e.g. dolphin's tail, Ollie's toothbrush). For plural words, that end in s, to show ownership, add an apostrophe after the s (e.g. teachers' staffroom).* Write four examples of an **apostrophe of ownership** of a **common** or **proper noun**. _____
   _____

4. *Can you remember the meaning of synonyms to complete this question?*
   Write the definition for **synonyms**: _____

5. There are three words relating to **motoring**. There is one **odd** word which relates to **a celebration once a year.** Find all **four** words:
   _____
   _____

b	i	r	t	h	d	a	y	i
g	e	a	r	s	t	i	c	k
s	n	o	a	l	a	d	e	p
l	q	p	e	t	r	o	l	c

6. What time does the teacher's clock show right now? _____
   What will be the time **5 minutes** from now? _____
   What **day** comes after Thursday? _____
   What **day** comes before Sunday? _____

   top row
   middle row
   bottom row
   left column   right column

7. 10 more than 5 385 = _____   100 more than 5 385 = _____
   1 000 more than 5 385 = _____

8. What **mode of transport** do you see at position right column, top row? _____

9. Circle and write the date of Australia Day. _____
   What **day** falls after 31 January? _____
   What **day** of the week will it be? _____

10. There are 8 light bulbs in a box, how many light bulbs did the hardware store have if they had 8 boxes left on the shelves? _____

10 Quick Questions a Day | www.lizardlearning.com

Year 4

Term 1 - Week 4 - Day 2

1. Rewrite the sentence/s with the correct **punctuation** and **spelling**.
   joke why was six afrad of sevin answer because sevin eight nine
   _____
   _____

2. *A phrase is a group of words without a verb. Many phrases start with a preposition.*
   Write a sentence that contains the phrase **towards me**. _____
   _____

3. *A prefix is a letter or group of letters placed before or in front of a word to change its meaning (e.g. un, re, mis).* Write four words that a **prefix** can be added to.
   _____ _____ _____ _____

4. *There are three articles: the, a and an. The, is a definite article (e.g. give me the cup). A, is an indefinite article (e.g. give me a cup. This would be any cup). An, is the article to use before a vowel (e.g. an umbrella).* Write the **articles** in the following sentence:
   A helicopter flew over the house. _____

5. Write the **consonants** in the **alphabet**. _____

6. What time does the teacher's clock show right now? _____
   What was the time **15 minutes** ago? _____
   20 months - 3 months = _____   **How many?** _____ years _____ months
   How many **days** in the current month? _____

7. Write the **value** of each underlined digit using words.
   1 9̲21 _____   4.3̲2 _____   2̲15 _____
   3̲.62 _____   8 38̲5 _____   6.5̲1 _____

8.
   ```
      5 8         7 _         8 _         4 _ 7       8 7 _       4 6 _
   +  6 _      +  6 4      -  4 2      -  1 6 3    -  1 _ 5    +  1 _ 8
      _ 1 9       1 _ 9       _ 5         _ 8 4       _ 5 1       _ 4 0
   ```

9. How **many** sessions of drawing? _____

10. Write a multiplication number story for the numbers 2 and 4.
    _____
    _____

5M's Art Group Timetable for Term One				
Activity	1.00pm	1.30pm	2.00pm	2.30pm
Face Painting - *Mr Beard*	Saturn	Mars	Earth	Neptune
Pottery - *Miss Potter*	Mars	Earth	Neptune	Saturn
Craft - *Mrs Simms*	Earth	Neptune	Saturn	Mars
Drawing - *Ms Curves*	Neptune	Saturn	Mars	Earth

Name:

Year 4 — Term 1 – Week 4 – Day 3

1. Rewrite the sentence/s with the correct **punctuation** and **spelling**.
   i cant wait until were home said millie because she was tird
   _____

2. Write the **dictionary** meaning for **submerge**. _____
   _____

3. *A suffix is a letter or group of letters placed after or at the end of a word to change its meaning.* Which word can use all four **suffixes**? -able / -s / -ed / -ing
   consider / wrong _____
   Write one of these new words in a sentence _____
   _____

4. Write the **nearest meaning** to **treasure**. _____
       a) a box that holds money and jewels   **b)** used to cover a bed

5. Write a word relating to **school** and then write the word in **past tense**.
   _____

6. What time does the teacher's clock show right now? _____
   What will be the time **10 minutes** from now? _____
   What is the missing **12 hour** time? _____ 11:20   11:40 _____ 12:20
   How many **months** have **30 days**? _____ Name them. _____
   _____

7. 4 groups of 5 fish: ___ x ___ = ___   2 x 13 = ___   0 x 18 = ___

8. Fill in this **picture pattern**.

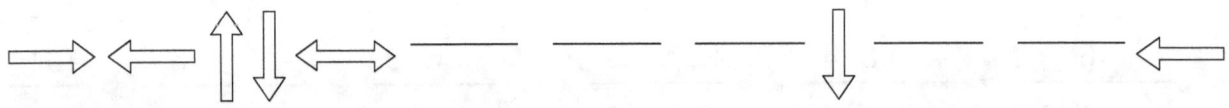

9. How many in the following? **horizontal** lines: _____ **vertical** lines: _____

10. Construction of the motel block was finished with just the carpet to lay. Joe laid the carpet in the foyer. 48 metres had to be laid on the first day, only 32 metres was laid. How much did he have left to lay? _____

Year 4

Name: _____

Term 1 - Week 4 - Day 4

1. Rewrite the sentence/s with the correct **punctuation** and **spelling**.
   ashley only had paint in red yellow and blu but new if she mixt these colours she culd make purple brown gren and even orang _____
   _____
   _____

2. **Can you remember the meaning of adverbs to complete this question?**
   Write the definition of **adverbs**. _____
   _____

3. **Compound words are two or more words joined together to form a new word (e.g. seashell).** Write a sentence that includes a **compound word**. _____
   _____

4. **A homograph is a word that has the same spelling but a different meaning (e.g. fine/fine) and sometimes a different sound (e.g. tear/tear).**
   Write two separate sentences using these **homographs**.
   cheek _____
   cheek _____
   block _____
   block _____

5. Write the words you find in this word worm. _____
   _____
   _____

   (word worm containing: plough, change, kettle, book, dress, cloak...)

6. What time does the teacher's clock show right now? _____
   What was the time **5 minutes** ago? _____
   65 months + 64 months = _____ **How many?** _____ years _____ months

7. Write the shaded **fraction** in numbers and words. _____

10 Quick Questions a Day | www.lizardlearning.com

21

8. **Draw** a **bar graph** using the information given.

9. Using 1 litre, 2 litres, 4 litres, 5 litres or more than 100L match the correct **measurement** to the picture

10. 110 pencils were bought by the group of students for use at their desks. There were ten desks. How many pencils for each desk? _____

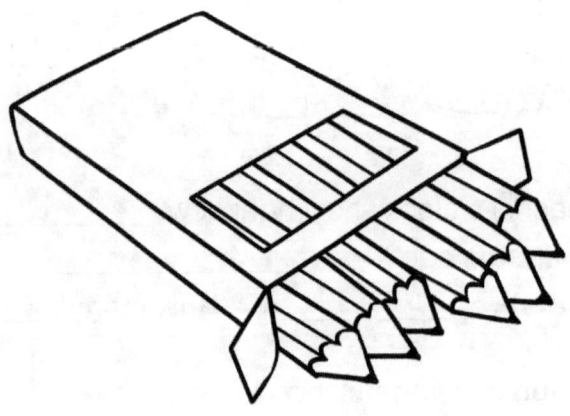

Year 4

Name:

Term 1 - Week 4 - Day 5

1. Rewrite the sentence/s with the correct **punctuation** and **spelling**.
   ahhh-chooo snezed caleb very lowdly i must be geting a cold
   _____
   _____

2. **Verbs are doing / action words.** Write four **verbs** that might occur at **dinner time**.
   _____

3. **Plurals are words that mean more than one.** Change **elf** to make it **plural**. _____

4. **Homophones are two or more words that sound the same but have different meanings and spelling (e.g. right/write).**
   Write four **homophones** and have someone write their matching **homophone**.
   _____ _____ _____ _____
   _____ _____ _____ _____

5. **Writing Time!** Finish this sentence: It was dark the moon was high when all of a sudden...
   _____
   _____ .

6. What time does the teacher's clock show right now? _____
   What was the time **30 minutes** ago? _____
   How many **days** in: Summer? _____ Autumn? _____

7. *Challenge!* If you bought the skateboard and the soccer ball, how much change would you have out of $100? Show your work: _____

8. **True** or **False**: 2 x 1 = 4 + 4 + 4 _____   half of 36 = 9 x 2 _____

9. **Volume is length x width x height. V = L x W x H. The symbol for cubic centimetres is abbreviated as cm3 (e.g. 3cm x 2cm x 7cm = 42cm³).**
   Challenge! How many **cubic centimetres** are there in this diagram? _____

10. 247 bricks were laid on the house. The brick layer had 221 more to go.
    How many bricks would he have laid altogether? _____

Year 4

Name:

Term 1 - Week 5 - Day 1

1. Rewrite the sentence/s with the correct **punctuation** and **spelling**.
   we are going on a tresur hunt for easta eggs in a fue weeks time the little girl excitedley told her brother _____
   _____
   _____

2. **Adjectives are describing words.**
   Write four **adjectives** that might occur **at the football**.
   _____ _____ _____ _____

3. **Contractions are shortened forms of two words.**
   We'll is a combination of which two words? _____

4. **Antonyms are words that are opposites.** Write an **antonym** for these words.
   sharp _____   after _____
   dangerous _____   large _____

5. **Rearrange** these words in **alphabetical** order. _____
   _____

   > someone   important   bought   structure

6. What time does the teacher's clock show right now? _____
   What will be the time **35 minutes from** now _____
   What is the missing **12 hour** time? 9:25 _____ 9:35 9:40 9:45 _____

7. **Doubles Facts (e.g. 2 + 2 = 4, 6 + 6 = 12).** Write the **doubles facts** for the twenties.
   _____ _____ _____ _____ _____
   _____ _____ _____ _____ _____

8. Complete these **fraction** number lines:

   0 — $\frac{2}{3}$ — 1 — $1\frac{2}{3}$

   0 — $\frac{1}{5}$ — $\frac{3}{5}$ — 1

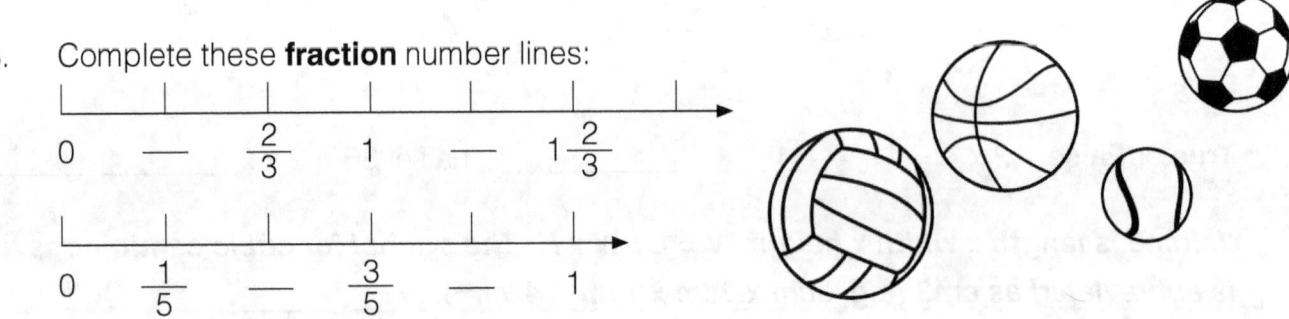

9. What **3D shape** does a ball make? _____

10. The farmer dug up 2 437 potatoes. He gave 437 to the cows how many did he have to take to the market? _____

Year 4 — Term 1 – Week 5 – Day 2

Name: _____

1. Rewrite the sentence/s with the correct **punctuation** and **spelling**.
   my pet birds name is max he enjoies nibling birdseed but his faverite chois is cuttle fish _____
   _____
   _____

2. **Can you remember the meaning of nouns to complete this question?**
   Write the definition for **nouns**. _____

3. Rewrite the misspelled words in this sentence:
   Mum was teachin Sally howe two maek scones. _____

4. **Synonyms are words that have similar meanings.** Write a **synonym** for these words.
   usual _____   wonderful _____
   smash _____   outgoing _____

5. **Rearrange** these words to make a proper sentence: Grandma up the picked to phone and it was call. my answer _____
   _____

6. What time does the teacher's clock show right now? _____
   What was the time **40 minutes** ago? _____
   25 months + 3 months = _____   **How many?** _____ years _____ months

7.
   ```
      6 4        4 2 3         3 5                    6 9 5 4
   +  1 9     + 3 1 2       - 2 9    Challenge!    -  1 2 1
   _____     _____       _____                 _____
   ```

8. Write the word that fits the sentence. **always / sometimes / never**
   Four horses will _____ gallop through the playground.

9. **Converting metres (m) to centimetres (cm) x 100.**
   Converting centimetres (cm) to metres (m) ÷ 100.
   Write as **metres** and **centimetres**. 502cm = ____m ____cm
   464cm = ____m ____cm   109cm = ____m ____cm   673cm = ____m ____cm

10. The golfer had 11 buckets of practice balls to hit at the driving range. In each bucket were 7 balls, how many balls did he have altogether? _____

10 Quick Questions a Day | www.lizardlearning.com

Year 4

Term 1 - Week 5 - Day 3

Name:

1. Rewrite the sentence/s with the correct **punctuation** and **spelling**.
   mim loved to go into the siti her favourite things to do were: shoping going to the movies and haveing a iced chocolate at a cafee _____
   _____
   _____

2. ***A pronoun is a word that takes the place of a noun (e.g. her, him, it, themselves).***
   Write a **pronoun** to take the place of: James _____, cake _____, elephant _____ .

3. These jumbled words are things that involve the **beach**.
   Rearrange them so they are spelled correctly. Are the words **nouns**, **verbs** or **adjectives**?
   tckbue _____ noun, verb or adjective? _____
   psade _____ noun, verb or adjective? _____

4. ***Can you remember the meaning of articles to complete this question?***
   Write the definition of **articles**. _____
   _____

5. Write the **odd** word out: | actor   actress   movies   claw | _____

6. What time does the teacher's clock show right now? _____
   What will be the time **45 minutes** from now? _____
   24 months + nine months = _____   **How many?** _____ years _____ months

7. 4 563 = _____ thousands _____ hundreds _____ tens _____ ones (ones)

8. Who sits **nearest** to the verandah and science experiments?
   _____
   Where would you like to sit? Why? _____
   _____
   _____

   WHITEBOARD
   FISH TANK | Billy | Tia | DOOR
   | Jed | Emma |
   | Oliver | Jasper | VERANDAH
   | Kate | Tina |
   SCIENCE EXPERIMENTS

9. Write these the **short way**:
   200 grams _____   365 grams _____
   19 centimetres _____   47 milimetres _____

10. Write a division number story for the numbers 16 and 4. _____
    _____
    _____

10 Quick Questions a Day | www.lizardlearning.com

Year 4

Name: _____

Term 1 - Week 5 - Day 4

1. Rewrite the sentence/s with the correct **punctuation** and **spelling**.
   the cats furr was long and silky-soft but the dogs hare was course and stringgy
   _____
   _____

2. *A preposition is a word used before a noun or a pronoun to show its relationship to some other word in the sentence; it is used to make a phrase (e.g. under the box, in the box, on the box, by, up, down, near, through, over, at).*
   Write the **prepositions** in this sentence: The lady left the shops and walked across the car park to her car. _____

3. *Apostrophe of ownership: for singular words to show possession of one owner, add an apostrophe then the letter s to the owner (e.g. dolphin's tail, Ollie's toothbrush). For plural words, that end in s, to show ownership, add an apostrophe after the s (e.g. teachers' staffroom).* Write four examples of an **apostrophe of ownership** of groups:
   _____ _____ _____ _____

4. Write the nearest meaning to **heavier**. _____
   a) a day of the week   **b)** an item that is not very light compared to another item

5. Rewrite this sentence in **future tense**: It rained a lot yesterday.
   _____

6. What time does the teacher's clock show right now? _____
   What will be the time **40 minutes** from now? _____
   Write the missing **12 hour** times: _____   8:30   8:45   _____   9:15   9:30   _____
   What **day** is before Friday? _____   What is **after** Tuesday? _____

7. *Calculator Sentences* - Change 420 to 20 using your calculator (e.g. 420 − 400 = 20).
   Write the **calculator sentence** to change **39** to **9**. _____
   Expand **4728**. _____
   _____

Year 4

Term 1 - Week 5 - Day 4

8. Using the coordinates **N**, **NE**, **NW**, **S**, **SE**, **SW**, **E** or **W**, complete the following statements:

   The Great Australian Bight is _____ of Tasmania.

   Tasman Sea is _____ of NSW

   WA is _____ of Indian Ocean

   QLD is _____ of NSW

   TAS is _____ of The Great Australian Bight

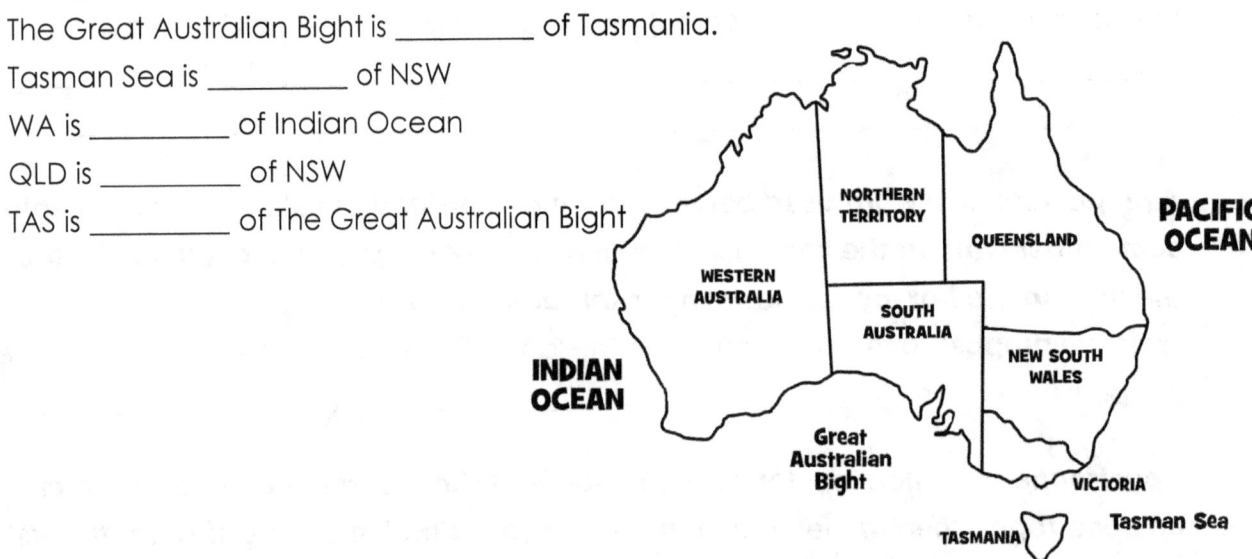

9. *An acute angle is less than 90 degrees. A right angle is 90 degrees. An obtuse angle is greater than 90 degrees but less than 180 degrees. A straight angle is 180 degrees exactly (a line). A reflex angle is greater than 180 degrees.*

   Which angle is a **right** angle? _____   Which is the **obtuse** angle? _____

   What **types of angles** are B and D? _____

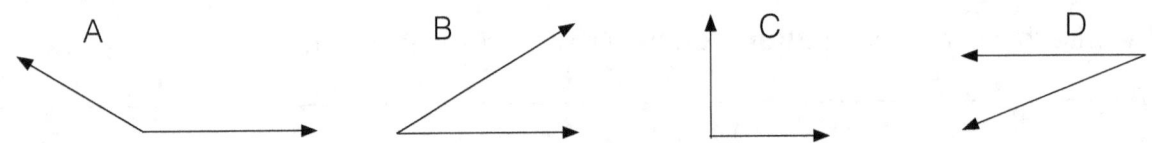

10. *Challenge!* Complete this magic square so each row, column and diagonal adds to **273**.

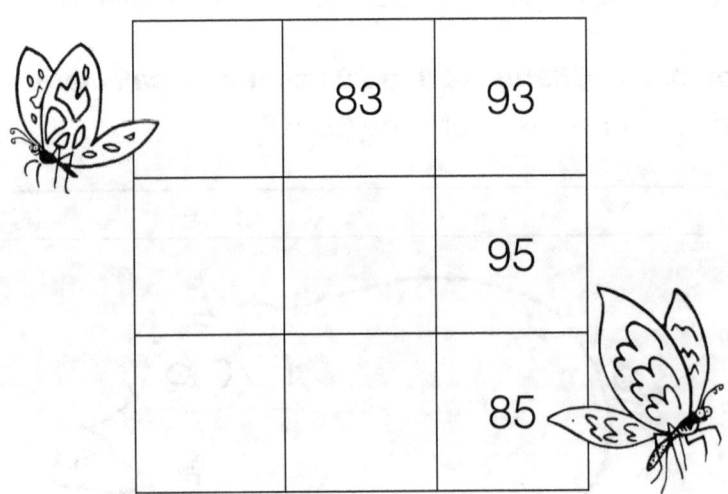

Name: _____

Term 1 – Week 5 – Day 5

1. Rewrite the sentence/s with the correct **punctuation** and **spelling**.
   do you ever have a dream in witch you are runnin very fast along the footpath wen all of a suddun you trip on the gutter and drop to the ground with a thud _____
   _____
   _____

2. *Can you remember the meaning of clauses to complete this question?*
   Write the definition of **clauses**. _____
   _____

3. *A prefix is a letter or group of letters placed before or in front of a word to change its meaning (e.g. un, re, mis).* Which word has the **prefix** that matches the meaning?
   To not have luck on your side. dislucky / relucky / unlucky _____

4. Is **buy** in this sentence a **homograph** or **homophone**? I asked Mum to buy me some more pencils when she goes to the store. _____

5. **Rearrange** these words to make a proper sentence:
   crashed string was hanging on broke. the when floor The it to the picture.
   _____
   _____

6. What time does the teacher's clock show right now? _____
   What will be the time **25 minutes** from now? _____
   51 months + 48 months = _____   **How many?** _____ years _____ months
   What **angle** is shown on the clock face now? _____

7. Use **numerals** and **decimals** to write: 4 tenths _____, 6 tenths _____.

8. Complete the **fraction** pattern:
   $\frac{2}{100}$ $\frac{4}{100}$ $\frac{6}{100}$ ____ ____ ____ ____ ____ ____ ____

9. What **day** and **date** was it 5 days before 11 April?
   _____
   Circle and write the **date** of Anzac Day: _____

10. There are 18 markers. At each point of a triangle, markers need to be placed evenly. How many markers will be placed at each point? _____

10 Quick Questions a Day | www.lizardlearning.com

Year 4

Name:

Term 1 - Week 6 - Day 1

1. Rewrite the sentence/s with the correct **punctuation** and **spelling**.
   all teachers favourite day is the last won befor sumer holidays
   _____
   _____

2. **A phrase is a group of words without a verb. Many phrases start with a preposition.**
   Write a sentence that contains one **phrase**. _____
   _____

3. **Contractions are shortened forms of two words.** Which word/s makes sense
   (**ocean, structure, until , use**) when you add **–ing** on the end? Rewrite the new words.
   _____

4. **Can you remember the meaning of homographs to complete this question?**
   Write the definition of **homographs**. _____
   _____

5. *Writing Time!* Finish this sentence: While walking through the park, there was a rustle in
   the bushes and … _____
   _____ .

6. What time does the teacher's clock show right now?_____
   What was the time **20 minutes** ago?_____
   23 months - 16 months = _____ months.

7. $438 $574 $361 $726 $869
   +$227   +$232   +$182   +$412   +$147
   _____   _____   _____   _____   _____

8. **Tally** this information.

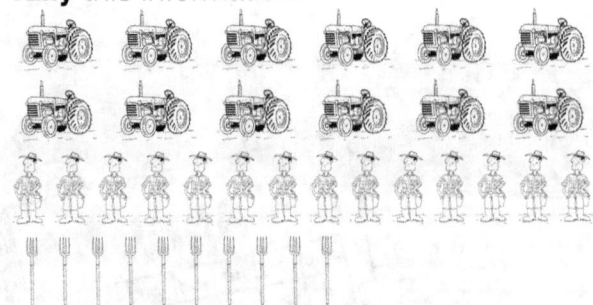

9. How many **vertical lines** are in the picture? _____

10. 801 ripe apples were on one tree and 111 on another.
    How many apples had to be picked that day? _____

10 Quick Questions a Day | www.lizardlearning.com

Year 4

Name:

Term 1 - Week 6 - Day 2

1. Rewrite the sentence/s with the correct **punctuation** and **spelling**.
   how many times hav u red the book charlie an the choclat factory sarah askd her frend lucy
   _____
   _____

2. Write the **dictionary** meaning for **hexagon**. _____
   _____

3. *Plurals are words that mean more than one.*
   Write **cleaners** in its **singular** form. _____

4. *Antonyms are words that are opposites.* Think of an **antonym**. Write a sentence with its opposite. Underline the **antonym** used. _____
   _____

5. Write these words in **alphabetical** order. _____
   _____

   cotton   dish   heard   duck

6. What time does the teacher's clock show right now? _____
   What will be the time **35 minutes** from now? _____
   Write the missing **12 hour** times.   8:35   7:35   6:35 _____   4:35 _____
   Before midday (am) or **after** midday (pm)?   8:00 coming to school _____
   2:00 asleep _____   3:00 finish of school _____   8:00 going to bed _____

7. **True** or **False**?   3 x 3 = 12 ÷ 3 _____   3 x 2 = 2 + 2 + 2 _____

8. = *equal to*   or   ≠ *not equal to*

   a) $\frac{1}{5}$ ___ ☐   b) 1 ___ $\frac{2}{2}$ c) ☐ ___ $\frac{1}{2}$ d) $\frac{3}{3}$ ___ $\frac{6}{6}$

9. What **time** does the Earth group start their face painting session? _____
   How **long** is each group session? _____

4M's Art Group Timetable for Term One				
Activity	1.00pm	1.30pm	2.00pm	2.30pm
Face Painting - *Mr Beard*	Saturn	Mars	Earth	Neptune
Pottery - *Miss Potter*	Mars	Earth	Neptune	Saturn
Craft - *Mrs Simms*	Earth	Neptune	Saturn	Mars
Drawing - *Ms Curves*	Neptune	Saturn	Mars	Earth

10. There were 1 766 tins of beans on the shelf. 59 tins had dents in them and could not be used. How many tins were good? _____

Name: _____

Term 1 – Week 6 – Day 3

1. Rewrite the sentence/s with the correct **punctuation** and **spelling**.
   doesnt she paint beautifully one artist sed too another
   _____

2. **Can you remember the meaning of nouns to complete this question?**
   Nouns are the names of _____, _____, _____, or _____

3. **Can you remember the meaning of compound words to complete this question?**
   Write the definition of **compound words**. _____
   _____

4. *Synonyms are words that have similar meanings.* Think of four **synonyms**.
   Test someone on their knowledge of synonyms that would match!
   _____ _____   _____ _____
   _____ _____   _____ _____

5. Write the words you find in this word worm. _____
   _____

6. What time does the teacher's clock show right now? _____
   What will be the time **50 minutes** from now? _____
   74 months - nine months = _____   How many? _____ years _____ months

7. **Numbers that end in 1 to 4 = round down.**
   Numbers that end in 5 to 9 = round up.
   Round these numbers to the nearest hundred.
   2 911 _____   3 882 _____
   4 733 _____   5 644 _____

8. What does the **abbreviation** QLD stand for?
   _____

9. **Redraw** this 2D shape as a **3D shape**.

10. *Challenge!* At the aquarium there were twelve tropical fish in each of 11 "Tropical Fish" tanks. How many fish were there altogether? _____

10 Quick Questions a Day | www.lizardlearning.com

Year 4

Term 1 – Week 6 – Day 4

1. Rewrite the sentence/s with the correct **punctuation** and **spelling**.
   joke why do bannanas hav to put on sunscreen befor they go to the beech
   answer becous they mite peal _____
   _____
   _____

2. **Verbs are doing / action words.** Write four **verbs** a **mouse** may do.
   _____ _____ _____ _____

3. **Contractions are shortened forms of two words.** Does this sentence use the **contraction** correctly? If not, fix it. Aun't you going to the movies this afternoon? _____
   _____

4. **There are three articles: <u>the</u>, <u>a</u> and <u>an</u>. <u>The</u>,** is a definite article (e.g. give me the cup). **<u>A</u>,** is an indefinite article (e.g. give me a cup. This would be any cup). **<u>An</u>,** is the article to use before a vowel (e.g. an umbrella). List the **article/s** in this sentence:
   The stove is very hot, so be careful or you will get a burn. _____

5. **Rearrange** these words to make a proper sentence: goes sister teddy My bear has a and to she everywhere likes take it. she _____
   _____

6. What time does the teacher's clock show right now? _____
   What will be the time **50 minutes** from now? _____
   27 months – 18 months = _____   **How many?** _____ years _____ months
   What **season** are we in now? _____

7. Circle the number that is the **smallest** in these groups of numbers.
   4 638 or 2000   7 987 or 3 000   2 765 or 7 000   3 000 or 5 674

8. Which **coordinate** shows a moon shape? _____
   What is the **shape** at 1,C? _____
   Which **coordinates** show the **face**? _____
   The **cloud** is on which **coordinates**? _____

9. **Volume is length x width x height. V = L x W x H.**
   The symbol for cubic centimetres is abbreviated as cm³
   (e.g. 3cm x 2cm x 7cm = 42cm³).
   How many **cubic centimetres** are in this diagram? _____

10. Write an addition number story for the numbers 578 and 220. _____
    _____

10 Quick Questions a Day | www.lizardlearning.com

Year 4

Name: _____

Term 1 – Week 6 – Day 5

1. Rewrite the sentence/s with the correct **punctuation** and **spelling**.
   the waves were so large they didnt just lap the side of the bout they actually sprayed all over the boots dek _____
   _____

2. **Adjectives are describing words.** Write the strongest **adjective** from this list.
   careful / cautious / watchful / wary _____

3. Correctly rewrite the misspelled words. Autum / Wintir / Sumer / Spring
   _____

4. Write the **nearest meaning** to **bought**. _____
           a) A verb to buy an item   **b)** To sing a tune

5. Write four words. Make one the **odd** one out. *Test someone near you.*
   _____ _____ _____ _____

6. What time does the teacher's clock show right now? _____
   What was the time **55 minutes** ago? _____
   Write the missing **12 hour** times. _____ 7:20 7:25 7:30 _____
   How many **weeks** in Autumn? _____ How many **months** in Autumn? _____

7. *Calculator Sentences - Change 420 to 20 using your calculator (e.g. 420 – 400 = 20).*
   Write the **calculator sentence** to change **45** to **5**. _____

8. Which shape are you **more likely** to pull out? _____

9. Using 1 litre, 10 litres, 100 litres or 1000 litres match the correct **measurement** to the picture.

   _____ L   _____ L

   _____ L   _____ L

10. Complete this magic square so each row, column and diagonal adds to **318**.

	98	108
102		
	104	100

Name:

Term 1 - Week 7 - Day 1

1. Rewrite the sentence/s with the correct **punctuation** and **spelling**.
   james was lookin for a pear of scissors so he heded for th kitchen drawer but all he could find wer tongs spoons and knifes _____
   _____
   _____

2. *An adverb is a word which modifies or adds meaning to a verb, adjective, or adverb by telling how, when, why or where a thing is done.* Write a sentence using one **adverb**.
   _____
   _____

3. These jumbled words are some of the states of **Australia**.
   Rearrange them so they are spelled correctly.
   eunlesndQa _____ wNe tSuho sWlae _____
   dlAaeade _____ mnaiasTa _____

4. *Homophones are two or more words that sound the same but have different meanings and spelling (e.g. right/write).* Write the correct **homophone** in this sentence:
   In the _____ (**passed** / **past**), television was seen in black and white.

5. Write the **vowels** in the following words: s c ___ ___ n c ___
   g ___ r d ___ n ___ n g   l ___ ___ v ___ n g   ___ ___ t b ___ c k

6. What time does the teacher's clock show right now? _____
   What will be the time **5 minutes** from now? _____
   93 months + 86 months = _____   **How many?** _____ years _____ months

7. *Ascending order is arranging numbers from smallest to largest.*
   Arrange in order from **smallest** to **largest**:   0.10   0.31   0.01   0.13   0.11   3.10   1.30
   _____

8. Which group of numbers shows counting **backwards** by **2's** _____
   a) 10, 9, 8, 7, 6   **b)** 60, 50, 40, 30   **c)** 28, 26, 24, 22   **d)** 30, 25, 20, 15

9. Approximate to the nearest **cm** the **length** of this line. _____
   ▬▬▬▬▬▬▬▬▬▬▬▬▬

10. One hundred and eight fish were bought and placed into bags of water.
    12 bags were needed. How many fish in each bag of water? _____

Year 4

Term 1 – Week 7 – Day 2

Name: _____

1. Rewrite the sentence/s with the correct **punctuation** and **spelling**.
   arent you feeling very well askd my fater when i came hom in teers
   _____
   _____

2. *Can you remember the meaning of pronouns to complete this question?*
   Write the definition of **pronouns**. _____
   _____

3. *Apostrophe of ownership: for singular words to show possession of one owner, add an apostrophe then the letter s to the owner (e.g. dolphin's tail, Ollie's toothbrush). For plural words, that end in s, to show ownership, add an apostrophe after the s (e.g. teachers' staffroom).* Write the **apostrophe of ownership/s** in the sentence:
   The boys bedroom had many pictures on the wall. _____

4. *A homograph is a word that has the same spelling but a different meaning (e.g. fine/fine) and sometimes a different sound (e.g. tear/tear).*
   Provide one example of a **homograph** at **Easter**: _____

5. Write the **past tense** for **give**. _____

6. What time does the teacher's clock show right now? _____
   What will be the time **10 minutes** from now? _____
   52 months + 46 months = _____   **How many?** _____ years _____ months
   How many **days** in **1 leap year**? _____

7. Isaac bought four chocolate bars.
   What was the **cost** of one bar? _____

   4 bars $8.00

8. How **tall** was the giraffe at birth on 19 December and again at 1 year later on 19 December?
   _____

   Giraffe's Growth (bar chart showing growth in metres measured on 19 Dec, 19 Mar, 19 Jun, 19 Sep, 19 Oct, 19 Dec)

9. Write the **short way**.
   25 grams: _____
   970 grams: _____
   641 kilograms: _____

10. $30 was the price of groceries at Buyless and $52 was the price of meat at the meat market. How much was spent on food altogether?
    _____

Year 4

Name: _____

Term 1 - Week 7 - Day 3

1. Rewrite the sentence/s with the correct **punctuation** and **spelling**.
   for his mums brthday he gave her a kiss a cudle and a botle of perfume
   _____
   _____

2. *A preposition is a word used before a noun or a pronoun to show its relationship to some other word in the sentence; it is used to make a phrase (e.g. under the box, in the box, on the box, by, up, down, near, through, over, at).*
   Write a sentence using one **preposition**. _____
   _____

3. *A prefix is a letter or group of letters placed before or in front of a word to change its meaning (e.g. un, re, mis).* Write the correct **prefix** from the box to match the word below.

   | re   un   pre | _____ lock

4. **Can you remember the meaning of antonyms to complete this question?**
   Write the definition for **antonyms**. _____

5. **Rearrange** these words to make a proper sentence: growing in the was over. The nicely knocked when it was pot plant _____
   _____

6. What time does the teacher's clock show right now? _____
   What was the time **15 minutes** ago? _____
   Write the missing **12 hour** times.   4:45 _____   5:45 _____   6:45
   Write **am/pm** for: I go to school in the _____ , I eat dinner in the _____ .

7. 3 x 3 = _____   3 x 6 = _____   3 x 6 = _____

8. Complete: Three thousand eight hundred and fifty-two plus _____
   equals three thousand nine hundred and fifty-seven

9. *An acute angle is less than 90 degrees. A right angle is 90 degrees. An obtuse angle is greater than 90 degrees but less than 180 degrees. A straight angle is 180 degrees exactly (a line). A reflex angle is greater than 180 degrees.*
   What **angles** does shape **A** have? _____

10. The truck was loaded with 7594 pumpkins. 117 fell off the truck.
    How many still left on the truck to take to the markets? _____

Year 4

Name:

Term 1 – Week 7 – Day 4

1. Rewrite the sentence/s with the correct **punctuation** and **spelling**.
   Summer was martins favorite seeson becuse he loved to swim surf and play criket
   _____
   _____

2. *A sentence or a clause, is a group of related words containing a subject and a verb.*
   Write one **clause** of your own. _____
   _____

3. *Can you remember the meaning of suffix to complete this question?*
   Write the definition of **suffixes**. _____

4. *Can you remember the meaning of synonyms to complete this question?*
   Write the definition of **synonyms**. _____

5. *Writing Time!* Finish this sentence: The fishermen were pulling up their nets but instead of fish there was ... _____
   _____

6. What time does the teacher's clock show right now? _____
   What will be the time **15 minutes** from now? _____
   87 months + 68 months = _____   **How many?** _____ years _____ months
   What **day** comes before: Sunday? _____   Tuesday? _____

7. **Odd** or **Even**?

8. What is the **chance** your teacher will smile at someone today?
   impossible, likely, possible or **certain**. _____

9. How **many** Saturdays in April? _____
   Circle the **date** of Good Friday:

10. Brisbane City Council runs 8 ferries up the Brisbane River per day. If there are 12 people on each ferry how many people were travelling altogether? _____

Year 4 — Term 1 – Week 7 – Day 5

Name: _____

1. Rewrite the sentence/s with the correct **punctuation** and **spelling**.
   the anstralian bilby is my favorite animal at easter time
   _____
   _____

2. Write the **dictionary** meaning for **pentagon**. _____
   _____

3. *Compound words are two or more words joined together to form a new word (e.g. seashell).* Write a **compound word** you would find **in the sky**. _____

4. Write the nearest meaning for **brought**. _____
       a) To cut food with   **b)** To bring something anywhere

5. **Rearrange** these words in **alphabetical** order. _____
   _____

       shaking   wizard   footsteps   window

6. What time does the teacher's clock show right now? _____
   What will be the time **25 minutes** from now? _____
   What are the missing **12 hour** times?   4:50   4:45 _____ 4:35 4:30 _____

7. *Calculator Sentences -* Change 420 to 20 using your calculator (e.g. 420 – 400 = 20).
   Write the **calculator sentence** to change **78** to **70**: _____
   Expand **6498**. _____

8. On the compass write **E**, **W**, **N** and **S**.

9. What **time** does Mrs Simms start her Neptune group on craft? _____

4M's Art Group Timetable for Term One				
Activity	**1.00pm**	**1.30pm**	**2.00pm**	**2.30pm**
Face Painting - *Mr Beard*	Saturn	Mars	Earth	Neptune
Pottery - *Miss Potter*	Mars	Earth	Neptune	Saturn
Craft - *Mrs Simms*	Earth	Neptune	Saturn	Mars
Drawing - *Ms Curves*	Neptune	Saturn	Mars	Earth

10. Write a subtraction number story for the numbers 625 and 112. _____
    _____

Year 4

Term 1 - Week 8 - Day 1

Name:

1. Rewrite the sentence/s with the correct **punctuation** and **spelling**.
   tania hadnt always loved pop music but these days she just thort it was the best. She was always being discovered danceing and singin along to her favorite songs buy her brothers
   _____
   _____
   _____

2. **Can you remember the meaning of phrases to complete this question?**
   Write the definition of a **phrases**. _____
   _____

3. **Plurals are words that mean more than one.** Rewrite these words in their **plural** form.
   apple _____   orange _____
   berry _____   banana _____

4. There are three articles: <u>the</u>, <u>a</u> and <u>an</u>. <u>The</u>, is a definite article (e.g. give me the cup). <u>A</u>, is an indefinite article (e.g. give me a cup. This would be any cup). <u>An</u>, is the article to use before a vowel (e.g. an umbrella). Write a sentence to include two **articles**.
   _____
   _____

5. Write the words you find in this word worm. _____
   _____
   _____
   _____

6. What time does the teacher's clock show right now? _____
   What will be the time **25 minutes** from now? _____
   34 months - 19 months = _____
   How many? _____ years _____ months

7. Write the number the **abacus** shows.
   _____

Name: _____

Term 1 - Week 8 - Day 1

8. What is located at 1,E? _____ What is at 3,C? _____
Write the **coordinates** of the park. _____
What are the **coordinates** of Cam's house? _____

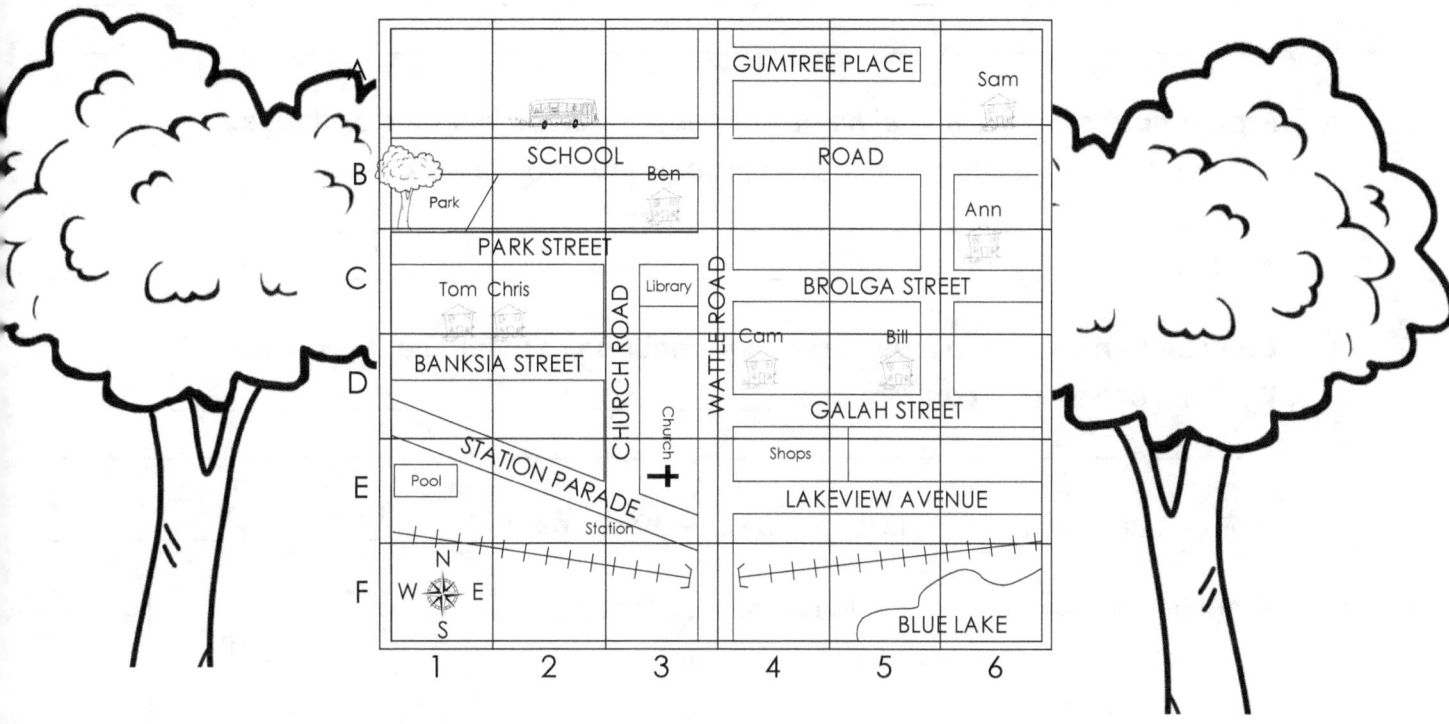

9. **Draw** an object that would weigh about 1kg:

10. Complete this magic square so each row, column and diagonal adds to **387**.

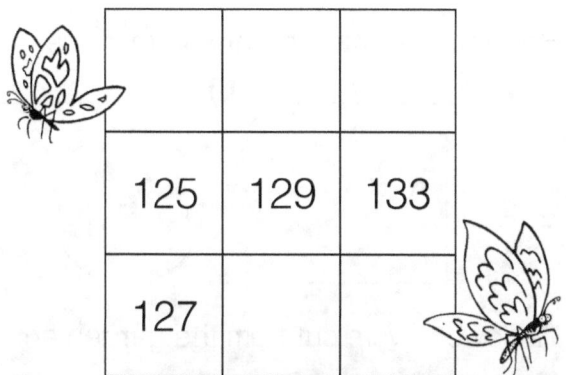

Year 4 — Term 1 – Week 8 – Day 2

Name: _____

1. Rewrite the sentence/s with the correct **punctuation** and **spelling**.
   lucas had many frends that he enjoied playin socca with at lunchtime among them where sam bill and john were his beest friends _____
   _____
   _____

2. *Proper nouns are the actual names of people, places, animals or things.*
   Write whether the following words are **proper nouns** or **common nouns**.
   Hobart _____ golf _____
   Aunty Sally _____ uncle _____

3. *Can you remember the meaning of contractions to complete this question?*
   Write the definition of **contractions**. _____
   _____

4. Provide one example of a **homophone** at **a theme park**. _____

5. There are three words relating to **nouns** that are **furry**.
   There is one **odd** word which relates to **time**.
   Find and write all four words. _____
   _____

d	n	o	c	e	s	p	a
n	r	k	o	a	l	a	i
f	e	m	u	s	s	o	p
h	b	u	n	n	y	l	o

6. What time does the teacher's clock show right now? _____
   What will be the time **30 minutes** from now? _____
   49 months + 46 months = _____ **How many?** _____ years _____ months
   How many **days** in Summer? _____ How many **weeks** in Summer? _____

7. Use decimals to write: 6 hundreds, 3 tens, 4 ones, and 1 tenth 9 hundredths _____

8. Complete this **picture pattern**.
   ____ 🐟 ____ 🐚 🐟 ____ 🐚 ____ 🪼 🐚

9. How many **horizontal lines** are in these shapes?
   a) _____   b) _____   c) _____   d) _____

   A (bracket shape) B (circle) C (triangle) D (double arrow)

10. 72 flowers were cut from the garden and they were to be placed into 8 vases.
    How many flowers for each vase? _____

Year 4

Name: _____

Term 1 – Week 8 – Day 3

1. Rewrite the sentence/s with the correct **punctuation** and **spelling**.
   come here come here he caled out to his dog as she run of with the tennis ball
   _____
   _____

2. ***Verbs are doing / action words.*** Write four **verbs** that apply to **a bird**.
   _____   _____   _____   _____

3. Correctly rewrite the **misspelled** words in this sentence: The old steem train rumbled down the trackes to the station. _____

4. ***A homograph is a word that has the same spelling but a different meaning (e.g. fine/fine) and sometimes a different sound (e.g. tear/tear).***
   Write two separate sentences to explain these **homographs**.
   date _____
   date _____
   dress _____
   dress _____

5. Write the **vowels** in the alphabet. _____
   Write the **consonants**. _____

6. What time does the teacher's clock show right now? _____
   What was the time **30 minutes** ago? _____
   57 months + 52 months = _____ **How many?** _____ years _____ months
   What **angle** does **8:00** show on a clock face? _____

7. How **much** money is shown? [coins/note] $_____
   Write in words: _____

8. How **many** children were surveyed? _____
   What was the **most popular** technology? _____

Technology at Home in 4P	
Laptop	|||| |||
iPod	||
iPad	|||| |||| ||
Wii	||||
Playstation	||||	

9. **Draw** the **top view** of these shapes:

   [cube]   [rectangular prism]   [cylinder]

10. Entry to the zoo was $63 for an adult and $24 for a child. How much did it cost the mother and her 2 daughters to gain entry to the zoo? _____

Name: _____

Term 1 – Week 8 – Day 4

1. Rewrite the sentence/s with the correct **punctuation** and **spelling**.
   you cant eat choclat every day and be sure youll still be helthy for example youre teath can becom very decayd from all the suger thats in choclate _____
   _____
   _____

2. *An adverb is a word which modifies or adds meaning to a verb, adjective or adverb by telling how, when, where or why a thing is done.* Write the **adverb** in the following sentence: The helicopter was swiftly patrolling the ocean for a lost swimmer. _____

3. **Unjumble** these words. The words in the box are spelled out correctly to help you.
   sutArliaa _____   ffgraie _____
   eecnsil _____   trcageeln _____

giraffe	rectangle
Australia	slience

4. *Antonyms are words that are opposites.* Write an **antonym** for these words.
   late _____   slow _____
   high _____   remember _____

5. Write if these sentences are **past**, **present** or **future tense**.
   The passengers will be getting off the ship. _____
   The passengers got off the ship. _____
   The passengers are on the ship. _____

6. What time does the teacher's clock show right now? _____
   What will be the time **40 minutes** from now? _____
   What are the missing **12 hour** times?   4:52 _____   4:56   4:58 _____

7. My answer is 10. I started with the number 20. What did I do for the answer to be 10?
   _____

8. 4 x _____ = 16   _____ x 2 = 12   10 x _____ = 20   _____ x 9 = 9

9. Which **3D** shape would this net make when glued together?
   _____

10. *Challenge!* The cherry farmer was picking his first crop of the season. He picked 366 cherries and he gave an equal amount of cherries to his 6 family members. How many cherries did each member of his family receive? _____

10 Quick Questions a Day | www.lizardlearning.com

Year 4

Name: _____

Term 1 – Week 8 – Day 5

1. Rewrite the sentence/s with the correct **punctuation** and **spelling**.
   In his mourning talk jeremy said atlantic puffins are the clowns of the sea he new this because his granddfather told him last weak _____
   _____
   _____

2. **Adjectives are describing words.** Write four examples of an **adjective**.
   _____ _____ _____ _____

3. **Apostrophe of ownership: for singular words to show possession of one owner, add an apostrophe then the letter s to the owner (e.g. dolphin's tail, Ollie's toothbrush). For plural words, that end in s, to show ownership, add an apostrophe after the s (e.g. teachers' staffroom).** Write four examples of an **apostrophe of ownership** of a **common** or **proper noun**. _____
   _____

4. **Synonyms are words that have similar meanings.** Write a **synonym** for these words.
   realise _____ sound _____
   fresh _____ scared _____

5. **Rearrange** these words to make a proper sentence: fed hand. The being his when the handler lost were alligators _____
   _____

6. What time does the teacher's clock show right now? _____
   What was the time **45 minutes** ago? _____
   44 months + 39 months = _____ **How many?** _____ years _____ months

7. Write the **odd** numbers from this list: 9 124   526   87   845   2 356   1 341   6 890
   _____
   Expand **6249**. _____

8. Using the words **least likely** and **most likely** what is the chance
   You will dye your hair tonight. _____
   Your Principal will come to school with a tie on. _____
   You will do sport this afternoon. _____

9. How many **right angles** does a square have? _____

10. The milkman delivered 6 crates of milk each containing 9 bottles of milk.
    How many bottles of milk did he deliver? _____

Year 4 — Term 1 - Week 9 - Day 1

Name: _____

1. Rewrite the sentence/s with the correct **punctuation** and **spelling**.
congratulations his parents called out from th frunt dor of his hom before he had even enteredthe gat _____
_____

2. **Can you remember the meaning of pronouns to complete this question?**
Finish this definition: Pronouns take... _____

3. **A prefix is a letter or group of letters placed before or in front of a word to change its meaning (e.g. un, re, mis).** Circle which word has the **prefix** that matches the meaning: to be sad or upset. A person could be: unsad / sadly / unhappy.

4. **There are three articles: <u>the</u>, <u>a</u> and <u>an</u>. <u>The</u>, is a definite article (e.g. give me the cup). <u>A</u>, is an indefinite article (e.g. give me a cup. This would be any cup). <u>An</u>, is the article to use before a vowel (e.g. an umbrella).** Write the **articles** in the following sentence: The little boy had a sore toe and had a bandage on it. _____

5. **Writing Time!** Finish this sentence: The bucket had a hole in it and the water was...
_____
_____

6. What time does the teacher's clock show right now?_____
What will be the time **35 minutes** from now?_____
36 months + 22 months = _____   **How many?** _____ years _____ months

7. What number are the **MAB blocks** showing? _____
Expand this number. _____

8. On the grid provided, **draw a sphere** at coordinate 2,B:

9. **Converting kilograms (kg) to grams (g) x 1000.**
Converting grams (g) to kilograms (kg) ÷ 1000.
Write **6 000 grams** as **kilograms**. _____

10. Write a multiplication number story for the numbers 4 and 3. _____
_____
_____

Year 4

Name:

Term 1 – Week 9 – Day 2

1. Rewrite the sentence/s with the correct **punctuation** and **spelling**.
   the childrin on the excurshion were told that dolfins can hold there breathe under warter for sevven minites before comeing up for air _____
   _____
   _____

2. *A preposition is a word used before a noun or a pronoun to show its relationship to some other word in the sentence; it is used to make a phrase (e.g. under the box, in the box, on the box, by, up, down, near, through, over, at).*
   Write the **preposition** you find in this phrase: outside the house _____

3. *A suffix is a letter or group of letters placed after or at the end of a word to change its meaning.* Write the correct **suffix** from the box to match the words.
   brave _____   notice _____   light _____ | en   able   ly |

4. Write the nearest meaning for **question**. _____
   a) To find information you ask this   **b)** To eat early in the morning before school

5. **Rearrange** these words in **alphabetical** order. _____
   _____
   should   police   reason   mean

6. What time does the teacher's clock show right now? _____
   What was the time **40 minutes** ago? _____
   What are the missing **12 hour** times?   _____   5:15   _____   5:45   6:00
   Write **am/pm** for: sport time _____   maths time _____   music time _____

7. **Calculator Sentences** - Change 420 to 20 using your calculator (e.g. 420 – 400 = 20).
   Write the **calculator sentence** to change 89 to 80. _____

8. Complete the pattern. Write the missing **fractions** on the lines.
   $\frac{67}{100}$ $\frac{69}{100}$ $\frac{71}{100}$ _____   _____

9. **Converting metres (m) to centimetres (cm) × 100.**
   Converting centimetres (cm) to metres (m) ÷ 100.
   Convert these **measurements** to centimetres.
   12.14m=_____ cm   14.03m=_____ cm   8.90m=_____ cm   16m=_____ cm

10. At the carnival, there were 63 students for each race with 7 lanes on the running track.
    How many students for each lane? _____

Year 4

Name: _____

Term 1 – Week 9 – Day 3

1. Rewrite the sentence/s with the correct **punctuation** and **spelling**.
   at the ice-cream shop theyre are so meny verieties of flavours today i sore chocolate chip strawbery caramal hokey pokey and vanila it was so difficult to make a choise _____
   _____
   _____
   _____

2. *A sentence or a clause, is a group of related words containing a subject and a verb.*
   Rearrange these words to make a **clause**: singing was stage. choir on the The
   _____

3. *Plurals are words that mean more than one.*
   Write four singular words and have someone write their matching **plural.**
   _____ _____ _____ _____

4. *Homophones are two or more words that sound the same but have different meanings or spellings (e.g. right / write).* Write two separate sentences using these **homophones**.
   stair _____
   stare _____

5. Write the words you find in this word worm. _____
   _____
   _____

   (word worm containing letters: taught, weigh, please, equal, laugh, grouser, cause, easter, robot, bottle)

6. What time does the teacher's clock show right now? _____
   What will be the time **45 minutes** from now? _____
   87 months + 52 months = _____ **How many** _____ years _____ months?

7. **Draw** any shape to show the **fraction** $\frac{1}{8}$.

10 Quick Questions a Day | www.lizardlearning.com

48

Year 4

Name: _____

Term 1 - Week 9 - Day 3

8. What state is the **largest**? _____
   What state is the **smallest**? _____

9. Do you know the **calendar rhyme**? Fill in the blanks.

   Calendar Rhyme
   30 days have _____, April, June and _____.
   All the rest have 31 except for February alone, which has 28 days clear but 29 days in each leap year.

10. Complete this magic square so each row, column and diagonal adds to **423**:

147	133	143
		145
		135

    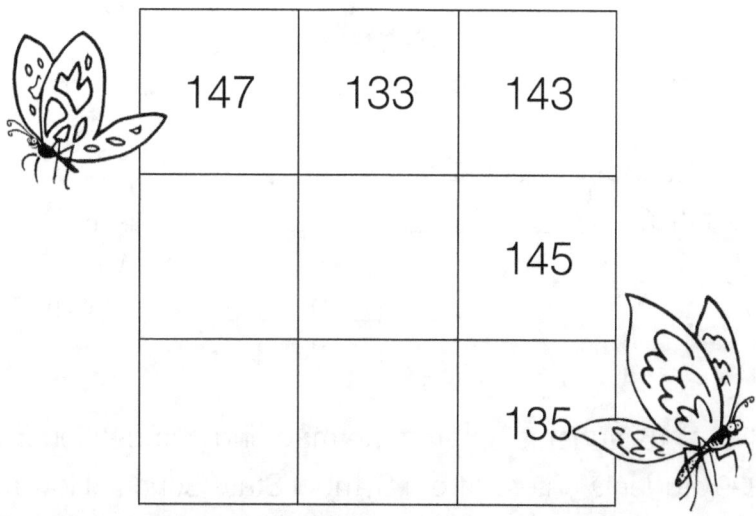

10 Quick Questions a Day | www.lizardlearning.com

Year 4

Name: _____

Term 1 - Week 9 - Day 4

1. Rewrite the sentence/s with the correct **punctuation** and **spelling**.
   she wondered how such a litle babie cud make so much nois
   _____
   _____

2. *A phrase is a group of words without a verb. Many phrases start with a preposition.*
   Write a sentence that contains one **phrase**. _____
   _____

3. *Compound words are two or more words joined together to form a new word (e.g. seashell).* Complete these **compound words**.
   _____ stairs   _____ end   _____ ball

4. *Can you remember the meaning of homographs to complete this question?*
   Write the definition of **homographs**: _____
   _____

5. Write the **odd** word out. | clock monkey dog animal | _____

6. What time does the teacher's clock show right now? _____
   What will be the time **50 minutes** from now? _____
   62 months - 12 months = _____ **How many** _____ years _____ months?

7. If you had $80 would you have enough to buy the dress? _____
   If so, how much **change** would I receive, if any? _____

   (shoes $39.90, dress $78.30, belt $19.95, shirt $60.50)

8. Write the **number** for the tally marks shown in this table.

Technology at Home in 4P		
Computer	𝍷𝍷𝍷𝍷 IIII	
iPod	II	
iPad	𝍷𝍷𝍷𝍷 𝍷𝍷𝍷𝍷 II	
Wii	IIII	
Playstation	𝍷𝍷𝍷𝍷 I	

9. Which letter has the **most** vertical lines? _____
   How **many** are there? _____

   A (square)   B (circle)   C (triangle)   D (double arrow)

10. At the Exhibition, 416 students entered the mapping competition from Lucinda State School and 399 students entered from Symbol State School. How many students entered altogether? _____

Year 4

Name: _____

Term 1 – Week 9 – Day 5

1. Rewrite the sentence/s with the correct **punctuation** and **spelling**.
   mum said too me twoday did you sea the sign at the shops that mentioned their were fireworks at the fare at samford tonight _____
   _____

2. *Adjectives are describing words.* Write the **dictionary** meaning for **mystery**. _____
   _____

3. *Contractions are shortened forms of two words.* Write the long version of the **contraction/s** in this sentence: If you can't see the bottom of the lagoon, you shouldn't dive into the water. _____

4. *Antonyms are words that are opposites.* Think of an **antonym**. Write a sentence with its opposite. Underline the **antonym** used. _____
   _____

5. Write the **vowels** in the alphabet. _____
   Write the **consonants**. _____

6. What time does the teacher's clock show right now? _____
   What will be the time **55 minutes** from now? _____
   What are the missing **12 hour** times?   12:10 _____   11:50 _____   11:30
   How many **days** in **6 weeks**? _____   How many **days** in **1 month**? _____

7. Find ten first then add the other numbers: 7 bottles, 3 caps, 8 lids. _____

8. **= equal to or ≠ not equal to**   10 less than 8 931 is ☐ 10 more than 88 913

9. How **long** does each session go for? _____

4M's Art Group Timetable for Term One				
Activity	**1.00pm**	**1.30pm**	**2.00pm**	**2.30pm**
Face Painting - *Mr Beard*	Saturn	Mars	Earth	Neptune
Pottery - *Miss Potter*	Mars	Earth	Neptune	Saturn
Craft - *Mrs Simms*	Earth	Neptune	Saturn	Mars
Drawing - *Ms Curves*	Neptune	Saturn	Mars	Earth

10. There were 4 093 surf competitors all lined up to race when the whistle blew. 247 broke and were disqualified. How many were left in the race? _____
    Spell your answer. _____

Year 4 — Term 1 – Week 10 – Day 1

Name: _____

1. Rewrite the sentence/s with the correct **punctuation** and **spelling**.
   the bridesmaids dresses was all made of silk and the brides dres was to
   _____
   _____

2. **Proper nouns are the actual names of people, places, animals or things.**
   Write four examples of a **proper noun**.
   _____   _____   _____   _____

3. Correctly rewrite the misspelled colours.
   purpul _____   oranj _____   gray _____   blew _____

4. **Synonyms are words that have similar meanings.**
   Think of four **synonyms**. *Test someone on their knowledge of synonyms that would match!*
   _____   _____   _____   _____
   _____   _____   _____   _____

5. Write if these sentences are **past**, **present** or **future tense**.
   I will be riding home from school. _____
   I rode home from school. _____
   I will be riding home tomorrow. _____

6. What time does the teacher's clock show right now? _____
   What was the time **40 minutes** ago? _____
   76 months + 22 months = _____   How many _____ years _____ months?

7. Write **31 592** in words. _____
   _____

8. Write the word that fits the sentence: | always   sometimes   never |
   Frogs will _____ be in your bed.

9. Using 250mL, 5 litres, 60mL or 10 litres match the correct **measurement** to the picture.
   (motor oil) ____ L   (bottle) ____ mL   (cup) ____ mL   (bucket) ____ L

10. Michelle has $1.30. That's twice as much money as I have. How much money do I have?
    _____

Year 4

Name: _____

Term 1 – Week 10 – Day 2

1. Rewrite the sentence/s with the correct **punctuation** and **spelling**.
   did you finesh your homework on time the techer ased the childen
   _____
   _____

2. **Can you remember the meaning of verbs to complete this question?**
   Write the definition of **verbs**. _____
   _____

3. **Unjumble** four spelling words from your weekly class list. *Test someone to see if they can work out your challenge!* _____
   _____

4. **Can you remember the meaning of articles to complete this question?**
   Write the definition of **articles**. _____
   _____

5. **Rearrange** these words to make a proper sentence: day. supermarket The closing for the was _____

6. What time does the teacher's clock show right now? _____
   What was the time **35 minutes** ago? _____
   41 months - 32 months = _____   How many **days** in April? _____

7. Write the place **value** of each underlined digit:
   6 29<u>3</u> = _____   8 <u>2</u>15 = _____   <u>9</u> 435 = _____

8. Write the coordinates of the **irregular pentagon**.
   _____

9. **Volume is length x width x height. V = L x W x H. The symbol for cubic centimetres is abbreviated as cm³ (e.g. 3cm x 2cm x 7cm = 42cm³).**
   How many **cubic centimetres** are in this diagram?
   _____

10. *Challenge!* Write a division number story for the numbers 7 and 12. _____
    _____
    _____

10 Quick Questions a Day | www.lizardlearning.com

Year 4

Name:

Term 1 – Week 10 – Day 3

1. Rewrite the sentence/s with the correct **punctuation** and **spelling**.
   their wasnt anyone else in the cinema so they had the pik of the saets
   _____
   _____

2. *Can you remember the meaning of adjectives to complete this question?*
   Write the definition of **adjectives**. _____

3. *Apostrophe of ownership: for singular words to show possession of one owner, add an apostrophe then the letter s to the owner (e.g. dolphin's tail, Ollie's toothbrush). For plural words, that end in s, to show ownership, add an apostrophe after the s (e.g. teachers' staffroom).* Write four examples of an **apostrophe of ownership** of groups:
   _____ _____ _____ _____ _____

4. Write the nearest meaning for **dozen**. _____
           a) A pack of 12   **b)** A keepsake in an album

5. *Writing Time!* Finish this sentence: The milk in the fridge was not good to drink as it...
   _____.

6. What time does the teacher's clock show right now? _____
   What will be the time **10 minutes** from now? _____
   What are the missing **12 hour** times? 5:15   5:10 _____   5:00 _____
   How many **weeks** in Term 1 of school? _____

7. *Calculator Sentences - change 420 to 20 using your calculator (e.g. 420 – 400 = 20).*
   Write the **calculator sentence** to change **145** to **463**. _____

8. Which ocean is **west** of Western Australia?
   _____
   What is **SE** of Victoria?
   _____

9. **True** or **false**? A table is the shape of a cone.
   _____

10. Sixty–six fish were bought and placed into bags of water. 6 bags were needed. How many fish in each bag of water? _____

10 Quick Questions a Day | www.lizardlearning.com

Name:

Term 1 – Week 10 – Day 4

1. Rewrite the sentence/s with the correct **punctuation** and **spelling**.
   The sho they wantid to sea was not sutable for children withot there parents permison so they couldnt go _____
   _____

2. *An adverb is a word which modifies or adds meaning to a verb, adjective, or adverb by telling how, when, why or where a thing is done.* Write the **adverb/s** in this sentence:
   The kitten was playfully jumping up on the scratching post. _____

3. *Can you remember the meaning of prefixes to complete this question?*
   Write the definition of **prefixes**. _____
   _____

4. *A homograph is a word that has the same spelling but a different meaning (e.g. fine/fine) and sometimes a different sound (e.g. tear/tear).* Which words are **homographs**.
   date _____ dress _____
   danger _____ evening _____

5. Write the words you find in this word worm. _____
   _____
   _____

6. What time does the teacher's clock show right now? _____
   What will be the time **45 minutes** from now? _____
   42 months + 12 months = _____ **How many** _____ years _____ months?

7. The recipe below will make one serving of Cocoa Mallow. You have two friends over that you know would enjoy this drink too. Rewrite this recipe so the three of you can share this drink together.

   ½ teaspoon cocoa powder   _____ teaspoon cocoa powder
   1 teaspoon of sugar   _____ teaspoons of sugar
   3 tablespoons of hot water   _____ tablespoons of hot water
   1 cup of milk   _____ cups of milk
   1 white marshmallow   _____ white marshmallows

8. Complete the **bar graph** using the results provided.

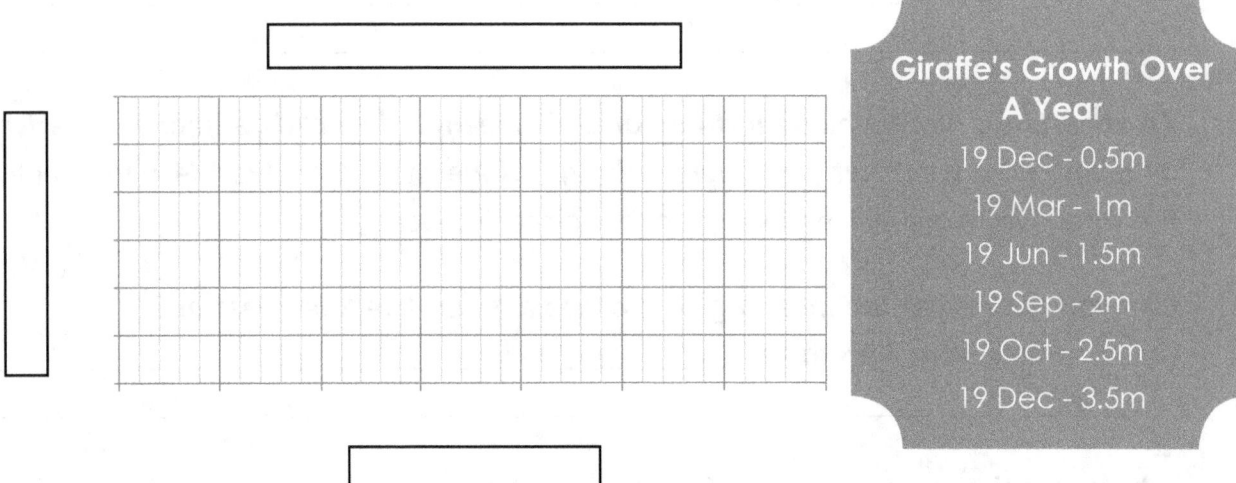

Giraffe's Growth Over A Year
19 Dec - 0.5m
19 Mar - 1m
19 Jun - 1.5m
19 Sep - 2m
19 Oct - 2.5m
19 Dec - 3.5m

9. Beside each picture write the appropriate **unit of measurement**, **grams** or **kilograms**.

_____   _____   _____

10. Complete this magic square so each row, column and diagonal adds to **477**.

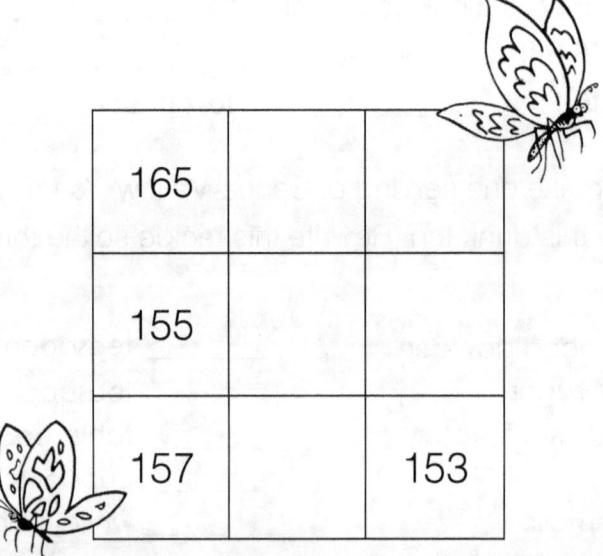

Year 4

Name: _____

Term 1 – Week 10 – Day 5

1. Rewrite the sentence/s with the correct **punctuation** and **spelling**.
   daniellas famely was from Italy so she wanted to go bak four a holidai
   _____
   _____

2. *A pronoun is a word that takes the place of a noun (e.g. her, him, it, themselves).*
   Write the correct **pronoun** into this sentence.
   It would be nice if _____ (you / yous / youse) would go together.

3. *A suffix is a letter or group of letters placed after or at the end of a word to change its meaning.* Which word has the correct **suffix**?
   very precious: breakable / unbreak / breakible _____

4. *Can you remember the meaning of homophones to complete this question?*
   Write the definition of **homophones**. _____
   _____

5. **Rearrange** these words in **alphabetical** order. _____
   _____

   > dozen   frozen   depart   wrong

6. What time does the teacher's clock show right now? _____
   What will be the time **50 minutes** from now? _____
   65 months + 34 months = _____ How many _____ years _____ months?

7. If you bought 2 soccer balls and a watch, how much would it cost? _____

   $15.50 $12.60 $33.70 $32.20

8. Which group of numbers shows counting **forwards** 4's _____
   a) 4, 40, 400, 4 000   b) 10, 40, 80, 120   c) 1, 2, 3, 4   d) 56, 60, 64, 68

9. Approximate to the nearest **cm** the **length** of this line. _____ cm

   ▬▬▬▬▬▬▬▬▬▬

10. Isaiah was a lumberjack. He cut down 349 trees on Monday and on Tuesday 483, how many trees had he cut down by Tuesday afternoon? _____

Name:

Answers

Week 1 - Day 1
1. "What would you like for dinner tonight?" Mum asked the family.
2. treasure, chest, bottom, sea
3. dislike
4. chilly
5. request, question, king, safely, seen, too, shadow, had, wade, deep
6. adult to direct, adult to check, 11 months, 14 days in a fortnight
7. $5.75, five dollars and seventy-five cents
8. △☆○△☆○△☆○△
9. motor oil - **2L**, milk carton - **1L**, bucket - **5L**, measuring jug - **250mL**
10. 8 mountaineers, 10 groups

Week 1 - Day 2
1. Sam loved to do all sorts of exercise, such as running, jumping, and even skipping.
2. was pushing
3. believe**d**, correct**ion**, slow**ly**, fresh**ly**
4. cheek, block, change
5. fruit
6. adult to direct, adult to check, 2 months, Thursday
7. various answers e.g.
8. Amber, Dyson, Floyd Eunice
9. 2cm³
10. 919 metres

Week 1 - Day 3
1. On the holidays, Josie visited Slippery Dip Aquatic Centre fifteen times.
2. blue
3. various answers e.g. swings, slippery slide
4. clean, under, no one, poor, sunny, far
5. **b**each, **r**emember**e**d, **b**efore, **b**ought, **c**omputer, **bl**ood
6. adult to direct, adult to check, 3:50, 3:55, **4:00**, 4:05, 4:10, various answers
7. 12, work: 24÷2=12
8. 2 more than 7 020 is **less than (<)** 2 more than 3 000 + 7 001
9. 8 faces, 12 corners
10. 505 metres

Week 1 - Day 4
1. The two boys' jackets were exactly the same.
2. happily, along
3. various answers e.g beach ball
4. closed - **shut**, seat - **chair**, near - **close**, laugh - **giggle**, small - **short**, jet - **aeroplane**
5. present, future, past
6. adult to direct, adult to check, 22 months, 10:00am - **before** / 4:10pm - **after**
7. nine thousand, two hundred and sixty-three
8. $\frac{2}{8}$ or $\frac{1}{4}$
9. 213cm, 434cm
10. 18 eggs, eighteen eggs

Week 1 - Day 5
1. Our footy team won in the finals between the Blue Birds and the Rugrats.
2. he
3. he is
4. a, the

5. We were at the pony riding school when one of our horses became frightened.
6. adult to direct, adult to check, 9 months, 100 years, December, January, February
7. 8 311, eight thousand, three hundred and eleven
8. 2,C, arrow
9. 50g, 116g
10. various answers e.g. There were 462 children in the school and another 214 enrolled. How many students altogether? 676 students

Week 2 - Day 1
1. "That dress is now half price so I might buy it," said Renee to Melissa.
2. on both layers, of the cake
3. sunny, dried, quickly
4. b
5. various answers, adult to check
6. adult to direct, adult to check, 5:55, 6:55, 7:55, **8:55**, **9:55**, **10:55** Right angle
7. 5 304, 6 901.2
8. (compass: N, W, E, S)
9. Obtuse: **A**, Acute: **B**, **D** C: **a right angle**
10. 9 screws

Week 2 - Day 2
1. At swimming lessons, we are learning backstroke, freestyle, butterfly and breaststroke.
2. The children were playing by the pool.
3. eelebiv - **believe**, ktabse - **basket**, rsidsate - **disaster**, utmnrgae - **argument**
4. witch / which, past / passed
5. aboard, medium, paw, quite
6. adult to direct, adult to check, 38 months, 3 years and two months, acute angle
7. no, $1.50
8. $\frac{35}{100}, \frac{40}{100}, \frac{45}{100}, \frac{50}{100}, \frac{55}{100}, \frac{60}{100}, \frac{65}{100}, \frac{70}{100}, \frac{75}{100}$
9. Monday
10. 282 flowers

Week 2 - Day 3
1. Jack's shirt was stained when he spilt his grape juice on himself.
2. under, In
3. girls'
4. homograph
5. break, care, careful, close, closed, to, crow, row, find, doctor, rabbit
6. adult to direct, adult to check, before, after, after
7. 1 cup desiccated coconut, 1 cup unsalted peanuts, 1 cup sunflower seeds, 1 cup sesame seeds, $\frac{3}{4}$ cup rolled oats, $\frac{1}{4}$ butter, $\frac{1}{2}$ brown sugar, $\frac{1}{4}$ cup honey
8. Ronan, Ali
9. 1:30pm
10.

29	15	25
19	23	27
21	31	17

Week 2 - Day 4
1. "Why did the teacher always look at her for the answer?" wondered Christie.
2. Willfully causing pain or suffering to another.
3. **dis**agree
4. various answers, adult to check e.g. cruel / kind
5. various answers
6. adult to direct, adult to check, **4:15**, 4:30, 4:45, 5:00, 5:15, **5:30**, 3 months
7. 12 eggs (1 emu egg + 9 duck eggs = 10 then 10 + 2 = 12 eggs)
8. 32 + 29 **not equal to (≠)** sixty-two, 147 **equal to (=)** 100 + 47, 28 + 12 **not equal to (≠)** 12 + twenty
9. A and C
10. 445 metres, four hundred and forty-five metres

Week 2 - Day 5
1. That wedding dress was so beautiful, I would like the same one when I get married.
2. various answers e.g. house, signpost, cars, dogs
3. happi**est**, various answers, adult to check
4. various answers
5. Vowels: a, e, i, o, u / Consonants: b, c, d, f, g, h, j, k, l, m, n, p, q, r, s, t, v, w, x, y, z
6. adult to direct, adult to check, 31 month = 2 years 7 months, 14 days
7. 3 000
8. various answer, adult to check
9. pump bottle - **50mL**, milk carton - **500mL**, can - **375mL**, glass bottle - **1L**
10. 63 pies, sixty-three pies

Week 3 - Day 1
1. Ipads come in lots of colours, such as red, black, white and yellow, but I prefer pink.
2. various answers, adult to check e.g. stack, sit, read
3. beaches
4. various answers, adult to check e.g. Sentences will use a, the, an
5. **teach:** taught, teach/teaches, will/shall teach
   close: closed, close/am closing, will/shall close
   film: filmed, film/am filming, will/shall film
   chase: chased, chase/am chasing, will/shall chase
6. adult to direct, adult to check, 28 months, 24 months
7. 3 065
8. circle, 3D shape
9. 3cm³
10. various answers e.g. I had 327 swap cards and I lost 238. How many have I now? 89

Week 3 - Day 2
1. The cake's icing was chocolate-flavoured so I ate it first.
2. various answers, adult to check e.g. big, loud, powerful
3. cook**top**, child**hood**, gate**way**
4. a
5. We were watching TV when a lizard walked in through the open door.
6. adult to direct, adult to check, 4:10, 4:12, **4:14**, 4:16, 4:18, **4:20**,

Year 4 — Answers

3 months
7. sum of 8 and 9 - **17**, product of 2 and 2 - **4**, one dozen plus six - **18**
8. Darwin / Northern Territory, South Australia and Western Australia
9. A
10.
43	29	39
33	37	41
35	45	31

Week 3 - Day 3
1. Allan didn't understand why his dad said he shouldn't walk around the backyard without shoes, until the day he stood on a thorn.
2. various answers, adult to check e.g. slowly, quickly, near
3. we are - **we're**, they are - **they're**, we will - **we'll**
4. reign - **rain**, scene - **seen**, right - **write**, sleigh - **slay**
5. various answers, adult to check
6. adult to direct, adult to check, 95 months, 7 years and 11 months
7. $\frac{1}{3}$, one third / $\frac{1}{2}$, one half, one half is bigger
8. C
9. 1cm
10. 12 plums

Week 3 - Day 4
1. Michelle was in trouble because her bike tyre was flat. She was very far from home and also from school, where she was headed.
2. you, I
3. square, sandwich, themselves
4. various answers e.g. bat/bat, project/project
5. however, invite, private, stung
6. adult to direct, adult to check, right angle
7. $100.40
8. Jane ||||| |||| - 9
   Ali || - 2
   Ronan ||||| ||||| || - 12
   Heather |||| - 4
   Tanisha ||||| | - 6
9. 2 000g
10. 547 children, five hundred and forty-seven children

Week 3 - Day 5
1. All the students' report cards were handed out on the last day of term.
2. various answers, adult to check e.g. beside, underneath, from, upon
3. various answers, adult to check
4. Antonyms are words that are opposites.
5. toward, between, outside, share, television, vision
6. adult to direct, adult to check, 4:00, 5:00, 6:00, **7:00**, **8:00**
7. First way - 2x0=0, 2x1=2, 2x2=4, 2x3=6, 2x4=8, 2x5=10, 2x6=12, 2x7=14, 2x8=16, 2x9=18, 2x10=20, 2x11=22, 2x12=24
   Turnaround - 0x2=0, 1x2=2, 2x2=4, 2x3=6, 2x4=8, 2x5=10, 2x6=12, 2x7=14, 2x8=16, 2x9=18, 2x10=20, 2x11=22, 2x12=24
8. South
9. C

10.
68	54	64
58	62	66
60	70	56

Week 4 - Day 1
1. "Can you think of a fruit beginning with K?" asked the teacher.
2. The Queen was sitting on her thrown.
3. various answers, adult to check e.g. teachers' staffroom, cat's whiskers, Cindy's house
4. Synonyms are words that have similar meanings.
5. 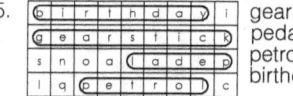 gearstick, pedal, petrol, birthday
6. adult to direct, adult to check, Friday, Saturday
7. 10 more than 5 385 = **5 395**
   100 more than 5 385 = **5 485**
   1 000 more than 5 385 = **6 385**
8. jetski
9. 26 January, 1st February Thursday
10. 64 lightbulbs

Week 4 - Day 2
1. Joke: Why was six afraid of seven? Answer: Because seven ate nine.
2. various answers e.g. The shark came towards me.
3. various answers e.g. (un) happy, (re) do, (mis) understand
4. a, the
5. b, c, d, f, g, h, j, k, l, m, n, p, q, r, s, t, v, w, x, y, z
6. adult to direct, adult to check, 17 months, 1 year and 5 months, various answers
7. 1 **9**21 - nine hundred,
   4.**3**2 three tenths, **2**15 - two hundred,
   3.62 - three ones (ones),
   8 3**8**5 - five ones (ones),
   6.**5**1 - one hundredth
8.
58	75	87	447	876	462
+ 61	+ 64	- 42	- 163	- 125	+ 178
119	139	45	284	751	640
9. 4
10. There were 4 pairs of socks on the line. How many socks altogether?

Week 4 - Day 3
1. "I can't wait until we're home," said Millie, because she was tired.
2. to place under water
3. consider / various answers e.g. We had a considerable amount of rain with the storm.
4. A
5. various answers, adult to check e.g. Study: I studied last night for my test on Friday.
6. adult to direct, adult to check, **11:00**, 11:20, 11:40, **12:00**, 12:20
   4 months, September, April, June, November
7. 4x**5**=20, 2x13=**26**, 0x18=**0**
8. ⇒ ⇐ ⇑ ⇔ ⇔ ⇑ ⇐ ⇐
9. horizontal - 3, vertical - 1
10. 16 metres

Week 4 - Day 4
1. Ashely only had paint in red, yellow or blue, but knew if she mixed these colours, she could make purple, brown, green and even orange.

2. An adverb is a word which modifies or adds meaning to a verb, adjective or adverb by telling how, when or where a thing is done.
3. various answers e.g. Football training was on the weekend.
4. various answers
   <u>cheek</u> - The baby had a spot on its <u>cheek</u>.
   <u>cheek</u> - Don't give me <u>cheek</u> the mother said to her mischievous child.
   <u>block</u> - The <u>block</u> was red and made of concrete.
   <u>block</u> - The girl had to <u>block</u> her face to stop the ball from hitting her.
5. plough, change, kettle, etch, book, zip, cloak, dress, dresser
6. adult to direct, adult to check, 129 months, 10 years and 9 months
7. $\frac{3}{10}$ / three tenths
8.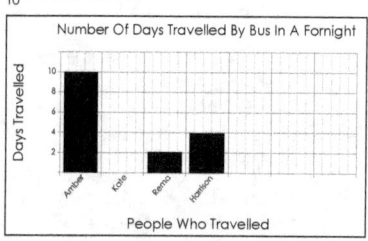
9. motor oil - **2L**, bucket - **5L**, pump bottle - **1L**, oil drum - **100L**
10. 11 pencils

Week 4 - Day 5
1. "Ahhh-chooo!" sneezed Caleb very loudly. "I must be getting a cold!"
2. various answers, adult to check e.g. eat, talk, sip, cut
3. el**ves**
4. Various answers, adult to check e.g. great/grate, break/brake, ate/eight
5. various answers, adult to check
6. adult to direct, adult to check, 90 days is Summer (91 leap year), 92 days in Autumn
7. **$50.80** / $33.70 + $15.50 = $49.20, $100 - $49.20 = $50.80
8. 2 x 1 = 4 + 4 + 4 - **false**
   half of 36 = 9 x 2 - **true**
9. 5cm³
10. 468 bricks

Week 5 - Day 1
1. "We are going on a treasure hunt for Easter eggs in a few weeks' time!" the little girl excitedly told her brother.
2. various answers, adult to check e.g. loud, large, high, smelly
3. we shall
4. sharp - **blunt**, after - **before**, dangerous - **safe**, large - **small**
5. bought, important, someone, structure
6. adult to direct, adult to check, 9:25, **9:30**, 9:35, 9:40, 9:45, **9:50**
7. 10+10, 11+11, 12+12, 13+13, 14+14
8. 0, $\frac{1}{3}$, $\frac{2}{3}$, 1, 1$\frac{1}{3}$, 1$\frac{2}{3}$
   0, $\frac{1}{5}$, $\frac{2}{5}$, $\frac{3}{5}$, $\frac{4}{5}$, 1
9. sphere
10. 2 000 potatoes

Week 5 - Day 2
1. My pet bird's name is Max. He enjoys nibbling bird seed, but his favourite choice is cuttlefish.
2. Nouns are the names of people, places, animals or things.

Year 4 Answers

3. teaching, how, to, make
4. various answers
   e.g. usual - **common**,
   wonderful - **astounding**, smash - **break**,
   outgoing - **friendly/sociable**
5. Grandma picked up the phone and it was to answer my call.
6. adult to direct, adult to check,
   28 months, 2 years 4 months
7.
64	423	35	1954
+ 19	+ 312	- 29	- 121
83	735	6	1833
8. various answers e.g. never
9. 5m 2cm, 4m 64cm, 1m 9cm, 6m 73cm
10. 77 balls

Week 5 - Day 3
1. Kim loved to go to the city. Her favourite things to do were: shopping, going to the movies and having an iced chocolate at a cafe.
2. James - **him/he**, cake - **it**, elephant - **it**
3. tckbue - **bucket** / noun
   psade - **spade** / noun
4. There are three articles: the, a and an. The, is a definite article (e.g. give me the cup). A, is an indefinite article (e.g. give me a cup. This would be any cup). An, is the article to use before a vowel (e.g. an umbrella).
5. claw
6. adult to direct, adult to check,
   33 months, 2 years 9 months
7. **4** thousands **5** hundred **6** tens **3** ones
8. Tina,
   various answers, adult to check
9. 200g, 365g, 19cm, 47mm
10. various answers e.g. 16 apples were arranged in 4 rows. How many in each row?

Week 5 - Day 4
1. The cat's fur was long and silky-soft, but the dog's hair was coarse and stringy.
2. across, to
3. various answers e.g. teachers' meeting, trees' leaves, childrens' swimming classes
4. B
5. It might rain a lot tomorrow.
6. adult to direct, adult to check,
   8:15, 8:30, 8:45, **9:00**, 9:15, 9:30, **9:45**,
   Thursday, Wednesday
7. 39 - 30 = 9,
   4 728 = 4 000 + 700 + 20 + 8
8. The Great Australian Bight is of **NW** Tasmania
   Tasman Sea is **SE** of NSW,
   WA is **E** of Indian Ocean,
   QLD is **N** of NSW,
   TAS is **SE** of Great Australian Bight
9. right - **C**, obtuse - **A**, B & D - **Acute**
10.
97	83	93
87	91	95
89	99	85

Week 5 - Day 5
1. Do you ever have a dream in which you are running very fast along the footpath, when all of a sudden you trip on the gutter and drop to the ground with a thud?
2. A clause is a group of related words containing a subject and a verb.
3. unlucky
4. homophone

5. The picture crashed to the floor when the string it was hanging on broke.
6. adult to direct, adult to check,
   99 months, 8 years and 3 months,
   adult to check
7. 4 tenths - 0.4 / $\frac{4}{10}$
   6 tenths - 0.6 / $\frac{6}{10}$
8. $\frac{2}{100}$ $\frac{4}{100}$ $\frac{6}{100}$ **$\frac{8}{100}$** $\frac{10}{100}$ $\frac{12}{100}$ $\frac{14}{100}$ $\frac{16}{100}$ $\frac{18}{100}$ $\frac{20}{100}$
9. Friday 6 April, 25 April
10. 6 markers

Week 6 - Day 1
1. All teachers' favourite day is the last one before Summer holidays.
2. various answers, adult to check
   e.g. Over the hill raced the boys.
3. structur**ing**, us**ing** (leave off the 'e')
4. A homograph is a word that has the same spelling but a different meaning (e.g. fine/fine) and sometimes a different sound (e.g. tear/tear).
5. various answers, adult to check
6. adult to direct, adult to check, 7 months
7.
$438	$574	$361	$ 726	$ 869
+ $227	+ $232	+ $182	+ $ 412	+ $ 147
$665	$806	$543	$1138	$1016
8.
Farm Names	
Tractor	||||‖ |||| ||
Farmer	||||‖ |||| ||||
Pitch Fork	||||‖ ||||
9. 11
10. 912 apples

Week 6 - Day 2
1. "How many times have you read the book Charlie and the Chocolate Factory?" Sarah asked her friend Lucy.
2. six sided shape
3. cleaner
4. various answers, adult to check
   e.g. sad/happy. She was happy after her dog had the pups.
5. cotton, dish, duck, heard
6. adult to direct, adult to check,
   8:35, 7:35, 6:35, **5:35**, 4:35, **3:35**,
   8:00**am**, 2:00**am**, 3:00**pm**, 8:00**pm**
7. 3 x 3 = 12 ÷ 3 - False
   3 x 2 = 2 + 2 + 2 - True
8. $\frac{1}{5}$ equal to (=)
   1 equal to (=) $\frac{2}{2}$
   ▨ equal to (=) $\frac{1}{2}$
   $\frac{3}{3}$ equal to (=) $\frac{6}{6}$
9. 2pm, 30 minutes
10. 1 707 tins

Week 6 - Day 3
1. "Doesn't she paint beautifully?" one artist said to another.
2. Nouns are the names of **people**, **places**, **animals** or **things**
3. Compound words are two or more words joined together to form a new word (e.g. seashell).
4. various answers, adult to check
   e.g. polite/considerate, over/above
5. violin, case, violin case, camp, church, chilly, crack, dirt, toe
6. adult to direct, adult to check,
   65 months, 5 years and 5 months
7. 2 911 - **2 900**, 3 882 - **3 900**,
   4 733 - **4 700**, 5 644 - **5 600**
8. Queensland
9. ▭

10. 132 tropical fish

Week 6 - Day 4
1. Joke: Why do bananas have to put on sunscreen before they go to the beach? Answer: Because they might peel.
2. various answers, adult to check
   e.g. squeak, hide, nibble
3. Aren't
4. the, a
5. My sister has a teddy bear and everywhere she goes she likes to take it.
6. adult to direct, adult to check,
   9 months, 0 years 9 months,
   various answers e.g. Brisbane in Term 1 is Autumn
7. 4 638 or (**2 000**), 7 987 or (**3 000**),
   (**2 765**) or 7 000, (**3 000**) or 5 674
8. moon shape - **2,A**, 1, C - **flower**,
   face - **2,B**, cloud - **1, B**
9. 6cm^3
10. various answers, adult to check
    e.g. Michael made 578 runs in the month of December and in January he scored another 220 runs. How many runs this Summer did he make altogether? 798 runs

Week 6 - Day 5
1. The waves were so large they didn't just lap the side of the boat, they actually sprayed all over the boat's deck.
2. various answers, discuss
3. Autumn, Winter, Summer
4. A
5. various answers, adult to check
6. adult to direct, adult to check,
   7:15, 7:20, 7:25, 7:30, **7:35**,
   12 weeks, 3 months
7. 45 ÷ 9 = 5
8. circle
9. fish bowl - **1L**, swimming pool - **1 000L**,
   bath tub - **100L**, trough - **10L**
10.
112	98	108
102	**106**	110
104	114	100

Week 7 - Day 1
1. James was looking for a pair of scissors, so he headed for the kitchen drawer, but all he could find were tongs, spoons and knives.
2. various answers, adult to check
   e.g. She ran home _fast_ to see her Easter present.
3. eunlesndQa - **Queensland**,
   wNe tSuho sWlae - **New South Wales**,
   dlAaeade - **Adelaide**,
   mnaiasTa - **Tasmania**
4. past
5. sc**ie**nce, g**a**rdening, l**ea**ving, **ou**tback
6. adult to direct, adult to check,
   179 months, 14 years and 11 months
7. 0.01, 0.10, 0.11, 0.13, 0.31, 1.30, 3.10
8. C
9. 7cm
10. 9 fish

Week 7 - Day 2
1. "Aren't you feeling very well?" asked my father when I came home in tears.
2. A pronoun is a word that takes the place of a noun (e.g. her, him, it, themselves).
3. boys' if there are more than one boy OR boy's if it is one boy

Answers

4. various answers, adult to check
   e.g. present/present
5. gave
6. adult to direct, adult to check,
   98 months, 8 years and 2 months,
   366 days in a leap year
7. $2
8. 19 December - **0.5 metre**,
   a year later - **3.5 metres**
9. 25g, 970g, 641kg
10. $82

Week 7 - Day 3
1. For his mum's birthday, he gave her a kiss, cuddle and a bottle of perfume.
2. various answers, adult to check e.g. On her birthday she hoped **for** a baby kitten.
3. **un**lock or **re**lock
4. Antonyms are words that are opposites.
5. The plant in the pot was growing nicely when it was knocked over.
6. adult to direct, adult to check,
   4:45, **5:15**, 5:45, **6:15**, 6:45,
   am, pm
7. $3 \times 3 = $ **9**, $3 \times 6 = $ **18**, $3 \times 9 = $ **27**
8. 105
9. A = right angle, one acute angle and two obtuse angles
10. 7 477 pumpkins

Week 7 - Day 4
1. Summer was Martin's favourite season, because he loved to swim, surf and play cricket.
2. various answers, adult to check
   e.g. The park was at her back door.
3. A suffix is a letter or group of letters placed after or at the end of a word to change its meaning.
4. Synonyms are words that have similar meanings.
5. various answers, adult to check
6. adult to direct, adult to check,
   155 months, 12 years and 11 months,
   Saturday, Monday
7. left -15 = **odd**, right - 23 = **odd**
8. various answers, discuss
9. 4 saturdays / various answers
10. 96 people

Week 7 - Day 5
1. The Australian Bilby is my favourite animal at Easter time.
2. 5 sided 2D shape
3. various answers, adult to check
   e.g. rainbow, sunbeam
4. B
5. footsteps, shaking, window, wizard
6. adult to direct, adult to check,
   4:50, 4:45, **4:40**, 4:35, 4:30, **4:25**
7. 78 - 8 = 70,
   6 000 + 400 + 90 + 8 = 6 498
8.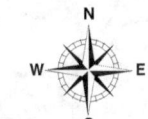
9. 1:30pm
10. various answers, adult to check
    e.g. There were 625 oranges in the orchard. After picking for one day there were 112 left. How many were picked?
    513

Week 8 - Day 1
1. Tania hadn't always loved pop music, but these days she just thought it was the best. She was always being caught dancing and singing along to her favourite songs by her brothers.
2. A phrase is a group of words without a verb. Many phrases start with a preposition.
3. apple**s**, orange**s**, berr**ies**, banana**s**
4. various answers, adult to check
   e.g. a, the, a
5. squid, different, liquid, ring, fair, graze, forgot, tongue
6. adult to direct, adult to check,
   15 months, 1 year 3 months
7. 5 721
8. 1, E - **pool**, 3,C - **library**, park - **1,B**, Cam's house - **4,D**
9. various answers e.g. butter container
10.
135	121	131
125	129	133
127	137	123

Week 8 - Day 2
1. Lucas had many friends that he enjoyed playing soccer with at lunchtime. Among them were Sam, Bill and John were his best friends.
2. Hobart - **proper**, golf - **common**,
   Aunty Sally - **proper**, uncle - **common**
3. Contractions are shortened forms of two words.
4. various answers, adult to check
   e.g. hi/high
5. 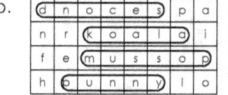 koala,
   possum,
   bunny,
   second
6. adult to direct, adult to check,
   95 months, 7 years, 11 months,
   92 days
   12 weeks in Summer
7. 634.19
8.
9. A - **1**, B - **0**, C - **1**, D - **2**
10. 9 flowers

Week 8 - Day 3
1. "Come here! Come here!" he called out to his dog as she ran off with the tennis ball.
2. various answers, adult to check
   e.g. fly, shake, eat, tweet
3. steam, rumbled, tracks
4. various answers
   date: We had a date to meet for coffee at 5pm.
   date: I loved to add a nice fresh date to my cereal in the morning.
   dress: My blue dress has flowers on it.
   dress: The nurse had to dress the wound when the patient came into the Emergency Centre.
5. vowels - a, e, i, o, u
   consonants - b, c, d, f, g, h, j, k, l, m, n, p, q, r, s, t, v, w, x, y, z
6. adult to direct, adult to check,
   109 months, 9 years and 1 month,
   obtuse angle
7. $6.05, six dollars and five cents
8. 33 surveyed, iPad
9.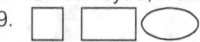
10. $111

Week 8 - Day 4
1. You can't eat chocolate every day and be sure you'll still be healthy. For example, your teeth can become very decayed from all the sugar that's in chocolate.
2. swiftly
3. sutArliaa - **Australia**, ffgraie - **giraffe**, eecnsil - **silence**, trcageeln - **rectangle**
4. late - **early**, slow - **fast**, high - **low**, remember - **forget**
5. future, past, present
6. adult to direct, adult to check,
   4:52, **4:54**, 4:56, 4:58, **5:00**
7. halved 20 or divided 20 by 2
8. 4x**4**=16, **6**x2=12, 10x**2**=20, **1**x9=9
9. cylinder
10. 61 cherries

Week 8 - Day 5
1. In his morning talk Jeremy said, "Atlantic Puffins are the clowns of the sea." He knew this because his grandfather told him last week.
2. various answers, adult to check
   e.g. sunny day, Winter morning, flat tyre, beautiful rainbow
3. various answers, adult to check
   e.g. table's legs, Easter bunny's egg, gardens' water systems
4. realise - **understand**, sound - **noise**, fresh - **new/recent**, scared - **afraid**
5. The alligators were being fed when the handler lost his hand.
6. adult to direct, adult to check,
   83 months, 6 years 11 months
7. 87, 845, 1 341
   6 000 + 200 + 40 + 9 = 6 249
8. various answers, discuss
9. 4 right angles
10. 54 bottles

Week 9 - Day 1
1. "Congratulations!" his parents called out from the front door of his home before he had even entered the gate.
2. Pronouns take **the place of nouns.**
3. unhappy
4. the, a, a
5. various answers, adult to check
6. adult to direct, adult to check,
   58 months, 4 years and 10 months
7. 4 072,
   4 000 + 70 + 2
8.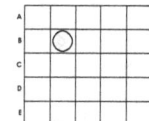
9. 6kg
10. various answers, adult to check
    e.g. 4 boys ate 3 Easter eggs each. How many Easter eggs did they eat?

Week 9 - Day 2
1. The children on the excursion were told that dolphins can hold their breath under water for seven minutes before coming up for air.
2. outside
3. brave**ly**, notice**able**, light**ly**/light**en**
4. A
5. mean, police, reason, should
6. adult to direct, adult to check,
   5:00, 5:15, **5:30**, 5:45, 6:00,
   various answers for all three next questions but they each will be either am or pm
7. 89 - 9 = 80
8. $\frac{67}{100}$ $\frac{69}{100}$ $\frac{71}{100}$ $\mathbf{\frac{73}{100}}$ $\mathbf{\frac{75}{100}}$

9. 1 214cm, 1 403cm, 890cm, 1 600cm
10. 9 for each lane

Week 9 - *Day 3*
1. At the ice-cream shop, there are so many varieties of flavours. Today I saw chocolate chip, strawberry, caramel, hokey pokey and vanilla. It was so difficult to make a choice.
2. The choir was singing on the stage.
3. various answers, adult to check
   e.g. table/tables, ice cream/ice creams, woman/women, man/men
4. various answers
   stair: The stair case was winding up to the ceiling.
   stare: Sometimes I stare into space when I'm thinking of new wiring ideas.
5. taught, weigh, please, equal, laugh, sauce, Easter, robot, bottle
6. adult to direct, adult to check,
   139 months, 11 years and 7 months
7.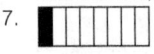
8. Western Australia, Tasmania
9. September, November
10.

147	133	143
137	141	145
139	149	135

Week 9 - *Day 4*
1. She wondered how such a little baby could make so much noise.
2. various answers, adult to check e.g The aeroplane was flying in the sky.
3. various answers, adult to check
   e.g. **up**stairs, **book**end, **basket**ball
4. A homograph is a word that has the same spelling but a different meaning (e.g. fine/fine) and sometimes a different sound (e.g. tear/tear).
5. clock
6. adult to direct, adult to check,
   50 months, 4 years and 2 months
7. Yes, $1.70
8. Computer ||||| |||| - 9
   iPod || - 2
   iPad ||||| ||||| || - 12
   Wii |||| - 4
   Playstation ||||| | - 6
9. vertical lines - **D**, how many - **4**
10. 815 students

Week 9 - *Day 5*
1. Mum said to me today, "Did you see the sign at the shops that mentioned there were fireworks at the fair at Samford tonight?"
2. something that is difficult or impossible to explain
3. can not, should not
4. various answers, adult to check e.g.
   Words that are opposites - mystery/fact
5. vowels - a, e, i, o, u
   consonants - b, c, d, f, g, h, j, k, l, m, n, p, q, r, s, t, v, w, x, y, z
6. adult to direct, adult to check,
   12:10, **12:00**, 11:50, **11:40**, 11:30,
   42 days
   28 (29 in a leap year) or 30 or 31
7. finding 7 and 3 equals 10 then 8 more = **18**
8. 10 less than 9 391 is **not equal to (≠)** 10 more than 88 913
9. 30 minutes or half an hour
10. 2 046 / two thousand and forty-six

Week 10 - *Day 1*
1. The bridesmaids' dresses were all made of silk, and the bride's dress was too.
2. various answers, adult to check
   e.g. Grand Canyon, Amazon River, Eiffel Tower, Mrs Cooper
3. purpul - **purple**, oranj - **orange**, gray - **grey**, blew - **blue**
4. various answers, adult to check
   e.g. words that are similar
5. future, past, future
6. adult to direct, adult to check,
   98 months, 8 years and 2 months
7. thirty-one thousand, five hundred and ninety-two
8. never
9. motor oil - **5L**, tomato sauce - **250mL**, measuring cup - **60mL**, bucket - **10L**
10. 65 cents

Week 10 - *Day 2*
1. "Did you finish your homework on time?" the teacher asked the children.
2. Verbs are doing / action words.
3. various answers, adult to check
4. There are three articles: the, a and an. The, is a definite article (e.g. give me the cup). A, is an indefinite article (e.g. give me a cup. This would be any cup). An, is the article to use before a vowel (e.g. an umbrella).
5. The supermarket was closing for the day.
6. adult to direct, adult to check,
   9 months, 30 days in April
7. 6 2<u>9</u>3 - **ones**, 8 <u>2</u>15 - **hundreds**,
   <u>9</u> 435 - **thousands**
8. 2,D
9. 6cm³
10. various answers, adult to check
    e.g. 72 children in Year 4 were placed into 12 rows for the Arts Council performance. How many children in each row? 6 children

Week 10 - *Day 3*
1. There wasn't anyone else in the cinema so they had the pick of the seats.
2. Adjectives are describing words.
3. various answers, adult to check
   e.g. trees' leaves, sheeps' wool, gardens' flowers
4. A
5. various answers, adult to check
6. adult to direct,
   adult to check,
   5:15, 5:10, **5:05**, 5:00, **4:55**,
   various answers e.g. 10 weeks
7. 145 + 318 = 465
8. Indian Ocean, Tasman Sea
9. False
10. 11 fish in each bag

Week 10 - *Day 4*
1. The show they wanted to see was not suitable for children without their parents' permission so they couldn't go.
2. playfully
3. A prefix is a letter or group of letters placed before or in front of a word to change its meaning (e.g. un, re, mis).
4. date, dress, evening
5. bulb, sharp, harp, smash, mash, shoot, hoot, sphere, history, story, koala

6. adult to direct,
   adult to check,
   54 months,
   4 years and 6 months
7. 1 ½ teaspoon cocoa powder,
   3 teaspoons of sugar,
   9 tablespoons of hot water,
   3 cups of milk,
   3 white marshmellows
8.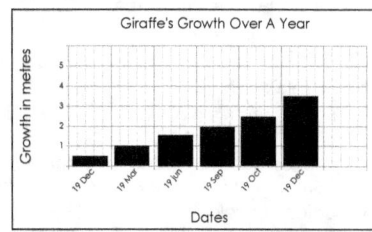
9. burger - **g**, man - **kg**, drink - **mL**
10.

165	151	161
155	159	163
157	167	153

Week 10 - *Day 5*
1. Danielle's family was from Italy so she wanted to go back for a holiday.
2. you
3. breakable
4. Homophones are two or more words that sound the same but have different meanings or spellings (e.g. right / write).
5. depart, dozen, frozen, wrong
6. adult to direct, adult to check,
   99 months, 8 years and 3 months
7. $63.20
8. D
9. 6cm
10. 832 trees

More Fun Resources

BOOTCAMP: PUNCTUATION & SPELLING

A series of resources designed to focus on essential Punctuation and Spelling skills.

RELIEF TEACHERS: 10 QUICK QUESTIONS A DAY - SURVIVAL GUIDE

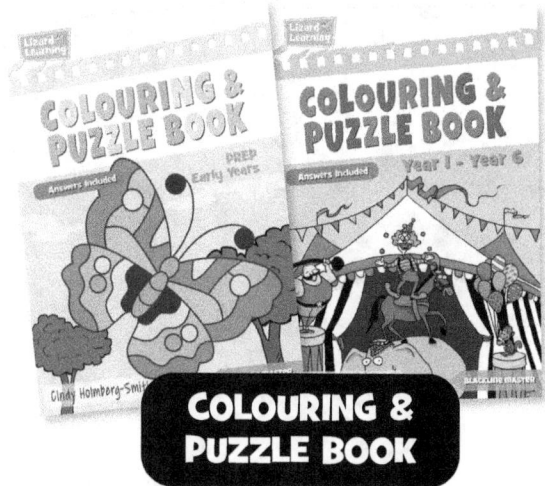

COLOURING & PUZZLE BOOK

Receive free activities and teaching resources delivered direct to your inbox plus be the first to find out about new time saving tools for teachers and exclusive offers.

www.lizardlearning.com

www.ingramcontent.com/pod-product-compliance
Lightning Source LLC
Chambersburg PA
CBHW050715090526
44587CB00019B/3393